ENDORSE

For decades Dr. Diehl has given encouragement and inspiration to thousands through his preaching ministry. Now, in this volume, we can relearn lessons he taught us through the reading of his sermonettes. I highly recommend *Refuel. Refresh. Revive* for renewed energy from our valued friend and mentor.

**—Dr. Loren Gresham, President Emeritus,
Southern Nazarene University, author**

During the COVID-19 pandemic Dr. Jim Diehl brought some sunshine into our lives with his weekly telecast. These pastoral moments have now been transcribed into this wonderful book *Refuel. Refresh. Revive.* I am pleased to give my strongest endorsement. Read and be blessed!

**—Dr. Tom Hermiz, General Superintendent Emeritus,
Churches of Christ in Christian Union, author**

Refuel. Refresh. Revive is a fitting title for this book from the heart and pen of a favorite preacher in Christendom. Dr. Jim Diehl has a gift in relating to the needs of readers and listeners. His writings have been shaped by down-to-earth experiences. While Dr. Diehl challenges people to a personal renewal in Christ, he "wraps the call in compassion and joy.

**—Dr. Nina Gunter, General Superintendent Emeritus,
Church of the Nazarene, author**

During the uncertainties of COVID-19 the voice of Dr. Jim Diehl was calming, encouraging, and reassuring. Thank God for these positive messages given during difficult days.

—Rev. Danny Goddard, senior pastor, author

From the heart of Pastor Jim Diehl comes this book of "life lessons." These lessons will encourage you, fill your mind with praise, and inspire you to "press on." Read them and be blessed!

—Dr. Connie Cunningham, wife of the late
Nazarene General Superintendent Paul Cunningham,
Church of the Nazarene; Bible teacher, mother, grandmother

During a very difficult time in our country and around the world, Dr. Diehl's *10 Minutes to Refuel* was a breath of fresh air. He is one of the best communicators, preachers, and storytellers I have ever heard. Each week we would wait with anticipation for the latest episode of a message that would challenge and change us. Now these messages are in print for all to read. Enjoy!

—Rev. Joe McNulty, senior pastor and counselor,
Cullman, Alabama

Always the gifted communicator, Jim Diehl has a style of presenting the powerful truths of Scripture that is framed within "spiritual common sense." His goal is immediate encouragement, hope, and application to everyday life. The "Diehl story" at the end of most chapters will bring a smile and perhaps laughter to the head and heart of the reader. It is my honor to recommend this book to every person of every generation.

—Rev. Mike Meeks, senior pastor;
Assistant to the District Superintendent,
Oklahoma District Church of the Nazarene

Dr. Jim Diehl's new devotional book, *Refuel. Refresh. Revive*, is loaded with inspiration and insights. The compassion from Dr. Diehl's loving heart spills onto each page, providing the reader with practical guidance. You will be encouraged as you taste the flavor of his unique writing!

—Dr. Norman Moore, evangelist, Church of the Nazarene

I have loved watching and listening to Dr. Diehl's wonderful *10 Minutes to Refuel* videos—I'm so happy to now have them in print! Every single one of them has made a difference for me; they are uplifting and inspiring—and they all bring the Word of God right down to where I live. If you're reading this book, you're truly holding a treasure.

—Cynthia Tobias, author and convention speaker

REFUEL REFRESH REVIVE

with PASTOR JIM DIEHL

dustjacket

Refuel. Refresh. Revive. / *Jim Diehl*

Published by Dust Jacket Press

ISBN: 978-1-95-328544-7

Dust Jacket Press
P.O. Box 721243
Oklahoma City, OK 73172

Interior design & cover production by D.E. West / www.zaqdesigns.com
with Dust Jacket Press Creative Services

CONTENTS

FOREWORD

Dr. Jim Diehl is truly a pastor of the people. His preaching over the years has always exuded his happy demeanor and Christ-like spirit. I have been privileged to be a part of many Jim Diehl preaching services and events, and I am always amazed at his gift of speaking effectively to any and all age groups. His stories are filled with practical wisdom and Spirit-directed insights that stay with you, working on your heart and mind for days to follow.

I have fond memories of the many conversations we have had over the years of our friendship. Jim once told me, "David, never forget that the Holy Spirit speaks through checks and prompts. Checks are the red lights in your spirit—Stop; watch; listen; warnings to be careful: 'Don't say that'; signs to change directions; bringing to mind a bad attitude or un-Christlike spirit. Prompts are green lights—Go; act; move; speak up; impressions to 'say this,' 'do this,' 'encourage them,' love. In this way the Holy Spirit will guide you in the way you should go."

Refuel. Refresh. Revive is full of many insights like this. Told in the way only Jim Diehl can, the sermonettes come alive in your spirit with the same vibrancy as if you were hearing them in a legendary Jim Diehl camp meeting sermon. As you read through these daily meditations, I believe your soul will be renewed in holiness, peace, and love. You will be encouraged, challenged, and inspired—and the Holy Spirit will speak to you through sacred checks and prompts.

—Dr. David A. Busic
General Superintendent
Church of the Nazarene

PREFACE

During the long COVID-19 pandemic of 2020–2021 most of the churches in North America were closed. Many pastors became creative and conducted services online, but many more churches just didn't have that ability or technical support—so their churches were silent. Many of my friends started talking to me about going online via Facebook and YouTube to bring encouragement to people of all faiths across North America and around the world. I finally launched into that ministry, calling it *10 Minutes to Refuel with Pastor Jim Diehl.* My son-in-law, Bernie Gitt, did the video work, and I brought the "sermonettes" for fifty-nine weeks.

I was amazed as to the number of people who tuned in and where they all lived—all across North America and a dozen countries beyond. After fifty-nine weeks the pandemic had somewhat lifted, churches were starting to meet in public worship again, and I felt that I had fulfilled the calling that the Holy Spirit had put on my heart to "stand in the gap" for just over one year. I didn't have a "sensational" listening/watching audience, but the average was between eight hundred to a thousand viewers per week. Come to think of it, that would be a great congregation even when the times were normal and healthy! I never ceased being blessed by the responses that came literally every week for over a year.

In recent times a number of people have asked if any of those "sermonettes" were in print. Of course, the answer was no. Then came an offer from a good friend who would listen to all fifty-nine and transcribe them into print. That has been done, I have edited each one to a degree (I found I don't preach in sentences or in paragraphs!), and the decision was made to have fifty of the fifty-nine put into a book. You will need to understand that these were not originally written out—rather, they were spoken. I trust they will flow smoothly as you read them, and possibly you can hear me preaching to my "online congregation."

I am not calling these "devotionals" on purpose. A devotional is a scripture taken and expounded on by the writer. These are more "sermonettes" to refuel, refresh, and revive your soul in the midst of your busy week. Of course, there is a scripture connected to each one and probably a short story or two to illustrate the truth, but read them with the understanding to "refuel" your spiritual gas tank.

My wife, Dorothy, was alive but slipping more and more deeply into the fog of dementia during those many weeks of filming. She would always sit in a chair near the camera and listen intently. Occasionally she would speak up and say something like "Jim, say that over again. I didn't quite get that." Of course, that meant we would stop, Bernie would reset the camera, and we would start in again. She is now in heaven and understanding far more than she could have ever understood or learned on *10 Minutes to Refuel.* Do I ever miss her! But there is a great reunion day coming! I plan on being at that reunion! I want to see you there too!

Therefore, keep your relationship with Jesus alive, and *He will get us all to the reunion,* which will last forever. Then we won't need to be refueled, refreshed, or revived! Thank the Lord! Don't miss the reunion!

ACKNOWLEDGMENTS

In early 2020 COVID-19 hit North America with a vengeance and the majority of the churches shut down their on-site public worship services. The idea was born in my heart to go on social media every week with *10 Minutes to Refuel with Pastor Jim Diehl* in an attempt to encourage and be a spiritual blessing to all who would listen or watch. The response was rather overwhelming! I continued that weekly communication for fifty-nine weeks and the numbers of those in my "virtual congregation" grew beyond hundreds into the thousands. To all of those who viewed the videos and wrote me asking for more, *I thank you!* That's the reason this book has been born—you kept asking me to put the sermonettes in print. Thank you for nudging me this direction.

Thank you to my son-in-law, Bernie Gitt (*gittphotography.com*), who videotaped every one of the fifty-nine editions of *10 Minutes,* put one of his great pictures with each one, and sent it off to YouTube. We spent many, many hours together in that production and he is now connected to this book project. The cover photo was taken by Bernie of a lonely church in the middle of the prairie well past midnight. When I saw that picture, I knew I wanted that one on the cover of the book.

Thank you to a very special friend in Oklahoma City who felt "burdened" to transcribe every one of the fifty-nine sermonettes into print. He has invested uncounted hours into this project and will continue to do so until the book is published. There is no way I could possibly pay you for your time invested! Thank you again!

Thank you to our son, Don, who has been very involved in organizing "who does what and when" along with Bernie. Don has also been responsible for setting up the website, along with our grandson Dalton. Don will also be the point person in marketing the book plus the "shipping and handling" of every order.

Thank you to each of our kids, Jodi, Jim, and Don, who got involved in this "book possibility" early on and have done a major amount of work behind the scenes. They have also offered a ton of encouragement to keep going, and I thank them for it.

Thank you to you whose stories and illustrations we were able to use in the book and how your stories contributed to this book. God bless you each.

Thank you to those who wrote to me in response to various sermonettes. I have quoted you in this book. My appreciation is given to Jeff Liles, Mark Murphy, Joe McNulty, Esther Crabtree, Danny Goddard, and Cindy Lamb. God bless you all!

Thank you to Adam Toler, president of Dust Jacket Press, for your expert guidance and counsel. You and your team are first class!

Thank you to Jonathan Wright, the final editor, who did amazing work to "make preaching readable."

Thank you to numerous other friends and relatives who have helped with everything from the title—*Refuel. Refresh. Revive*—to getting the spoken word translated into the written word. I deeply appreciate you all and I pray that God will bless all our efforts to challenge, lift, and encourage people across North America and around the world.

1 MOTHER GOOSE AT BEAR CREEK PARK

Psalm 91

Greetings to you from the Jim and Dorothy Diehl home in Lakewood, Colorado. We are in the middle of Holy Week. Good Friday and Easter Sunday are coming. Something happened to us a few years ago, just two days after Easter, that I want to tell you about—just a little story, and it certainly has a scriptural connection to it.

Here's what happened. Something happened to my wife, Dorothy, and her heart started acting up terribly. She ended up being taken to the emergency room in an ambulance and then was admitted to the hospital. She had congestive heart failure, and before the whole thing was over, it was eight days in the hospital and a new heart valve and other things too complicated to tell.

Right in the middle of that, I received a report from the urologist that I had a cancerous tumor in my bladder. They had taken biopsies of that, and the report came back from the lab: "high-grade cancer, very aggressive."

That didn't sound very good to me; I don't like anything about cancer, but that put a little scare into me. With my wife in the hospital with a major heart problem, I took our little puppy dog, Kasey, got him on the leash, and we went out about five or six minutes from home to a little park called Bear Creek Park. Nice lake there and a few people, but a whole lot of Canada geese. At this time of the year evidently it was the time that the female geese were giving birth to their little goslings, and I'll probably just call them chicks—that's just easier. We saw this Mama Goose, and then Papa Goose was right by her; he was kind of her bodyguard. Two little chicks were following along, and I said, "Oh, man—that's the picture we need," so I got my iPhone camera out. Kasey was getting kind of a kick out of this, and he wanted to get up and say something to these little chicks, I think. I got a little too close, and I mean that Mama Goose put her wings out as wide as a goose can get them and started hissing at me.

I kind of thought it was funny, so I wanted to get in and get a little closer picture, while directly she must have given a signal to those little chicks, because they ran into her, and those big wings folded over those two little chicks and I could not see a foot—I could not see a thing except a mama goose with her wings tight. So I took the picture, but it was no good, because it was just a picture of a mama goose. How would you know that her two little chicks are on the inside?

I turned to walk away and was thinking about all of that, and maybe eight, nine, or ten steps away I saw a feather on the ground. That's pretty typical, I guess, with that many geese around, but I picked it up and looked at it. I felt as if the Holy Spirit of God whispered in my ear, "That's what I want to do for you and Dorothy. I want you to come on in close to me now and let me cover you with my feathers—and under my wings you will be safe."

Well, I headed for home, and as you know, there are a lot of scriptures about God's wings and "under his feathers," so I checked every one of them out. Of course, this is the one I like the best and probably the one you might know. Psalm 91—"He who dwells in the secret place of the Most High shall abide under the shadow of the Almighty. I will say of the Lord, 'He is my refuge and my fortress; My God, in Him I will trust.' Surely He shall deliver you from the snare of the fowler. . . . He shall cover you with His feathers, and under His wings you shall take refuge" (vv. 1–4).

"There it is! If you and Dorothy will come on in and get under my wings, I'll take care of you."

Well, I started thinking about that. Those two little chicks under the wings of Mama Goose. What was happening to them? They were safe; they were secure; they were protected; they were all right!

I want to tell you today—when we had the pandemic going on from the coronavirus, and it was terrible, terrible, terrible, I want you to know that God does not want you to ever live in fear. It says in the very next verse, "You shall not be afraid of the terror by night, nor of the arrow that flies by day, nor of the pestilence that walks in darkness, nor the destruction that lays waste at noonday" (vv. 5–6). *Do not be afraid!*

Now I want to say that I think we ought to use our heads. So I had my mask and I used that when I went out, and I think that was just being sensible and trying to use the brain that God gave me. But my hope and trust is not in the mask but in the Almighty God who has us underneath His wings!

The next morning I got up, opened the shades of our bedroom, looked down (because we're on the second floor), and there in our backyard I saw something. I got dressed, went out to the backyard, and in the grass was a feather! It was a different one, not the one I had found the day before. It was not lying on the ground—it was sitting straight up. I've lived here five or six years and had never seen a feather in the yard—ever! And I haven't seen one since. As I picked up that feather, I really believe the Lord winked at me and said, "What do you think of that, son? What do you think of that?"

I said, "Lord, I can't imagine."

So now I have two feathers. I don't worship these feathers, but they're symbols to me that God is taking care of us, and God will take care of *you*! By the way, Dorothy's heart was okay, and my last report on the bladder was all clear, all clean—thanks be to God! I want to tell you during the wonderful Easter week, resurrection Sunday, or anytime—get under the wings of God and take refuge and don't fear. God is bigger than any situation! God is bigger than "What's the matter?" *Get under His wings!*

2 GOD SPOKE TO ME!

Acts 8:29

Last Saturday I had an email from a wonderful couple up in Wisconsin I've met at various church events and retreats. They live in Green Bay now. These are good people and friends, but we don't talk back and forth very much. I think maybe since Christmas I've heard from them one time, so that's why this is a bit surprising to me. The email came just a few days ago. "You have been on my wife's mind so much the last two days that we had to send a note. Praying for you." Then they talked about some things and closed, "Stay well, dear friends. God bless," and signed the email.

They had no way of knowing that on Thursday of last week I had oral surgery on two teeth: one upper one and one lower one that had to be removed by the oral surgeon. Those teeth had been in there since I was a little boy, and they didn't want to come out. I think you have an idea that it was a tough day. Then they had to do the bone grafting to get ready for implants that are going to come someday. Thursday was a pretty difficult day. On Friday I think I had a reaction to the pain medication because I was a little bit tipsy, spacy, and nauseous, and everything else so that was not a really good day either. By Saturday I was starting to get better, and then this email came.

How in the world did she know that I was going through two very difficult, painful days? There's only one way—the Lord impressed me upon her mind and that she ought to be praying extra for me. I thought that was wonderful. That's so common, but you know I just thought it was special that God did that so that she could help me through the thing, not even knowing what the problem was.

When we look back into the Scripture—I'm going to the book of Acts here today—it seemed it was common for the early Christians to be talking about the Spirit with a capital S: "The Holy Spirit said to me . . ." It's all through the book of Acts, but let's just start right here in chapter 8, verse 29: "Then the Spirit said to Philip, 'Go near and overtake this chariot.'" Now I just wrote out some things so we'll just kind of go a little quicker that way. In Acts 10:19 we read, "The Spirit said to him [Peter]" and the words following in chapter 11, verse 12, "The Spirit told me to go," and another one in chapter 11: "Agabus . . . showed by the Spirit," of course, capital S, the Holy Spirit. In Acts 13:2 we read, "The Holy Spirit said, 'Now separate to Me Barnabas and Saul.'" In Acts 16:6 we read, "They were forbidden by the Holy Spirit to preach the word in Asia" and then several more times it was common to read, "the Spirit said," "the Spirit led," "the Spirit . . ." The Scripture says they were forbidden by the Holy Spirit to preach in Asia. Sometimes the Spirit says, "Go," sometimes "No." Sometimes it's a green light, sometimes a red light!

If we who really believe that Jesus Christ is Lord, He lives in our hearts, within us, and God is a God of love. I think we all agree to that. If He's a God of love, He doesn't want us to live a religion of rules or a religion of rituals—He wants a relationship with us. If God wants a loving relationship with me and you, *don't you think he wants to talk to us once in a while?* Sure—that's part of a relationship.

Here's what happened. I was on the plane from Denver to Philadelphia sitting in the window seat, the middle seat was open, and in the seat by the aisle was a young lady, maybe in her 30s. I didn't know her at all. The flight took off and we were somewhere over middle America. I was doing whatever I was doing, and I felt a nudge.

I felt a prompt: "Give the lady your $50 bill."

I said, "Lord, no. I'm not going to give her that $50 bill. I don't know the woman."

"Give the lady your $50 bill."

I said, "Lord, I'm not used to going up to ladies and saying, 'Hey—I'll give you $50 here.'" You know, you're going to get in trouble sooner or later doing that.

So I said, "Lord, don't. No, no"

"Give the lady your $50 bill."

I finally got my billfold and pulled out my $50 bill, touched the lady on her arm, and said, "Ma'am, I don't know you and you don't know me, and I'm a little embarrassed to do this, but I felt impressed to give you this fifty-dollar bill."

Immediately her eyes welled up in tears and she said, "I knew God was in this. I knew God was in it."

I said, "God's in what?"

"My mom. My mom has a brain tumor and she's going into surgery on Monday. My mom is not a believer—she's not a Christian. I need to go and try to help Mom to get right with God before she goes into brain surgery, but we didn't have the money for the trip, so my husband and I said we're going to put it on the credit card. This $50 doesn't pay for the whole thing, but it tells me that God's in this. God's in this!"

Well, by then my eyes were bubbling up in tears. I said, "God bless you. Let's pray for your mom," which we did.

We got to Philadelphia, said goodbye, and that's the end of that. I had that prompt. I had that nudge of the Spirit and said yes, and that was it.

The Spirit spoke to me about a month later. I was out on Kipling Street, which is just west of us here, coming back home, and I drove by Walgreens. I don't go to Walgreens much (I go to another pharmacy), but in some way I felt led to go to Walgreens. I was standing in line in order to pay, and somebody came up behind me and said, "Rev. Diehl, is that you?"

I turned around, and so help me, it was the lady who was on the plane. I said, "Hey—what are you doing here?"

"Oh," she said, "I've got to tell you; I've got to tell you about Mom. She gave her heart to the Lord, and she said, 'I'm going to be meeting God. I want to know He's my Savior!' She had the surgery; she came through wonderfully well. I was there a week, and when I came home, the last thing Mom said was 'I gave my heart to Jesus because I thought I was going to die; now that I'm going to live, I'm going to live for Jesus!'"

This lady from the plane was just nearly jumping up and down and said, "God was in it! God was in it! And you had a part in it."

I could do nothing other than wipe my own tears and say, "Thank you, Jesus. How you can do that, Lord, I don't know."

Do you think my going into Walgreens was a coincidence? No, that was divine providence, for God to get me in there to buy two or three things, to see the lady—and I've never seen her since!

God just wanted me to know the end of the story. How about you today? You'll feel prompted or you will feel nudged to call somebody, to text somebody, to email somebody, maybe to share this story with two or three or more. It's wonderful when we feel that nudge of the Spirit and then we say, "Yes, Lord." Good things happen! God bless you. Live for Jesus!

3 ONLY GOD CAN DO THAT!

Acts 12

As I've been praying this week about this time together, I felt drawn to telling you a story or two about an "only God can do that" kind of a miracle. For the biblical account, of course, there are a few hundred of these types of miracles in the Word.

I've chosen the one out of Acts chapter 12. Instead of reading it, here's the story briefly told. It was the early church, the New Testament church. Herod was the king. He was over all this area of Jerusalem and beyond and had to keep these Jews under control. He knew they disliked this band called Christians, so wicked Herod had James, one of the leaders of the early church, killed with the sword. Then the Bible says that when he saw that had pleased the Jews, he said, "Well, I'll also go after the main man, Peter."

So he had Peter, who was the leader of the early church, arrested and put in prison until after Passover, which was in just a few days. By then Jerusalem would be filled with people because of the big feast time and all the other events surrounding Passover. He was going to bring Peter out of prison and have a "trial," and then that would be his day of execution. That would make the Jews happy forever, and Herod would be solidly on his throne.

The Bible says that the night before Peter was to be brought out, an all-night prayer meeting took place over at the home of Mary, the mother of John Mark. They were praying, "O God—we can't lose any more. Lord God, set Peter free."

In the middle of the night God sent an angel to the prison. Now, I'm going to put this in USA English. The angel said to Peter, "Get up, get dressed, and get out of here." Peter got up. The Bible says that he was chained on both hands to two different guards; those chains fell off. The guards did not hear or see a thing. Peter got dressed. The angel (Peter did not think it was an angel—he simply thought he was seeing a vision) led him out of that prison. They came to the big iron gate that opened to the city; that iron gate opened to them of its own accord. Peter walked out of the prison in the middle of the night. I'm sure he had to turn around and look at the prison and probably said something like this: "I'm going to die someday, but I'm not dying tomorrow at the wicked hand of Herod—praise be to the Lord!" That is a miracle of "only God can do that."

He turned and headed toward Mary's home, where the prayer meeting was being held. Their prayers had been answered because "only God can do that."

Here's how I've been feeling impressed: a whole lot of you reading this need an "only God can do that" kind of miracle, or answer to prayer, if you prefer. I want your faith to rise! We serve a great God! The God who got Peter out of prison—that's the God we serve! I don't want you to be like what J. B. Phillips wrote in his book *Your God Is Too Small*! Come on—let's let our faith rise here today! God is big enough to give you an "only God can do that" kind of answer to prayer.

Now I have one story to tell you. I likely have a hundred—but time for only one. Here's the one I feel led to tell. It was our first church, in Muscatine, Iowa, a small church. I don't think anybody starts with a big one. We got into that ministry but we needed some more people. The few we had were overworked and there were just too many problems that I don't think I had better talk about. We were praying, "O God, you've got to send us some more people. Lord, we've got to have more horses to pull the load around here." To make a long story short, God sent us a family. They moved in because the father was working on the new interstate just north of us; his name was Skeeter Brown. He, his wife, and the kids were wonderful Christians. They loved the Lord and they loved this church. Once they got in, she became the leader of our youth, and it was such an answer to prayer. Skeeter could fix anything that would break or quit working. He was "Mr. Fix-it" for everything, and the family's spirit was so encouraging. The whole church took a spark because of this family.

Well, for a year or two it was good, the church was growing, and they fit in just perfectly. Everything was going right—until one Sunday night after the service when Skeeter came to me with his head kind of hanging down and said, "Preacher, we've got to move. They're transferring me to the west side of Iowa. I've got to move."

"No, no, no, Skeeter. You can't! This whole thing—it's just perfectly fitting together."

"I don't want to move," he said, "but I'm being transferred."

I went over to our home (the parsonage) heavyhearted. I said, "Lord, isn't there any way?" I went to sleep a very troubled preacher. Oh, you hate to lose people, especially good ones like that.

You won't believe this, but here's what happened. Monday morning Skeeter Brown was on my front porch dinging the bell. I went to the door and said, "Skeeter, what are you doing here?" I'm not making this up—one of his eyes was swollen shut. I said, "What's the matter with your eye?"

He said, "Preacher, on the way home last night I just prayed,

'Lord, if you don't want us to move and you need us in this church, close one eye.'" I've never heard that one in my life. His eye was swollen shut. He said, "Come on—get in the car. We're going to go out and find a job for me today." We went south of Muscatine, and you know, that's on the Mississippi River, and we found a place where there was a great big dragline.

He told me, "I know how to run those things." We went up over a road and got down—this dragline was being shaken. We got out of the car. Skeeter yelled up at the guy and asked, "Do you know how to run that thing? "

The man looked down and said, "No, I own it, but I don't know how to run it. Look—the man who runs the thing left me and I'm trying to figure it out."

Skeeter said, "Would you like for me to come up and show you?" He crawled up into the cab, got that thing going, and it was soon swinging around doing everything.

Skeeter came back down, and the owner said, "Would you like to have a job?"

Skeeter said, "I'm looking for one."

The man said, "When can you start?"

Skeeter said, "I better give them a week. I can start a week from today."

We got in the car, headed back for home, and he looked at me and said, "Only God can do that!"

You may not believe me, but when we got home his eye had opened. That is an "only God" miracle. For the rest of our time there, what a blessing they were!

I want to tell you today that God still lives! That's our God! He got Peter out of prison in the middle of the night! And the miracle that I just told you is absolutely word-for-word true!

We're in a tension in this country; we're in tension everywhere. I believe God is saying that it's time for a "only God can do this" kind of a miracle and answer to prayer for you and for me. Let's pray that way. God bless you all.

4 TEMPTATIONS, TRIALS, AND TESTS

1 Corinthians 10:13

I'm sure that the chapter of life I'm in currently affects which scriptures really jump out at me. I'm now the chief caregiver for my wife, Dorothy, who has the dreaded disease of dementia. Life is different for me now, so you can understand why at the time I came on the following scripture about a week ago, I just stopped and read it again and again. It's 1 Corinthians 10:13: "No temptation has overtaken you except such as is common to man; but God is faithful, who will not allow you to be tempted beyond what you are able, but with the temptation will also make the way of escape, that you may be able to bear it."

I read that, but I thought, "I don't feel as though I'm in a period of heavy temptation. I sense that it's more of a testing time, more of a trial that both Dorothy and I are going through." Therefore, I added two more words, *trial* and *test*, plus *tried* and *tested*, and wrote them into those verses: "No temptation [trial or test] has overtaken you except such as is common to man; but God is faithful, who will not allow you to be tempted [tried or tested] beyond what you are able, but with the temptation [trial or test] will also make the way of escape, that you may be able to bear it." If any of you are living anywhere near where I live in life's journey, it's just not temptations that wear you down—it's also the trials of life and it's the testing times that God allows us to go through.

Even Jesus went through trials, tests, and temptations. Twice in my life I've gone through a period that the theologians call "the dark night of the soul." That is when, spiritually speaking, everything goes dark and it seems that you're in a fog.

One of those times lasted a month and the other lasted for six weeks. I was a pastor of a good church, and everything was going great at the church. It was not that some people were acting up. No, I don't have any idea why this testing time came, but it seemed that my joy was gone. I felt that my peace had the London fog over it. It seemed that everything that could go wrong did go wrong. I remember that something went wrong with the car, something went wrong with some of the appliances in the house, the telephone quit, and I said, "Well, *you* just might as well quit too—everything else is breaking down."

Thank the Lord—God seemed to lift the heaviness while I was trying to preach. But about the time I got back home from church, that "dark night of the soul" would settle on me again, and I said, "Lord, what have I done or what am I doing? What's wrong?" I looked up what scholars and theologians said about "the dark night of the soul" and found out that it's not uncommon. In fact, it's common to most of us somewhere and sometime in life.

I got where I could hardly take anymore darkness, so I went out to a nearby lake, Lake Keomah, that was rather secluded and started walking and praying. I walked the path telling the Lord, "I've had about all this darkness and heaviness that I could take." I do remember that since nobody was around, I just hollered out, "Lord, my name is not Job! Lord, get me out of this valley!" I can't explain it, but out at that lake in the woods the Lord lifted the heaviness and confusion—and I was set free!

Do you know what I preached that next Sunday morning? You know what I preached! The title: "When Your Sky Goes Black." I told them that I had been going through a dark time, the sky had been dark, and I hadn't sensed the peace or joy of the Lord for six weeks. I told them about my trip out to Lake Keomah. I told them about my crying and saying, "My name is not Job!" I told them how God lifted the darkness from me and the presence of Jesus Christ returned to my heart.

In the Church of the Nazarene we have altars at the front of the sanctuary, and those altars are great places for Christians to pray as well as for sinners. I said, "If any of you are going through a dark time, come to the altars." They almost flooded the front of the church, and people were kneeling in more places than the altars could hold. I remember going back and forth praying for each one. These were my people and I called them by name. "Lord, Lord—push the darkness out!" One lady put her hand out and stopped me. I won't forget what she said: "Pastor, your darkness lasted for six weeks. Mine has lasted for six *months.* Pray for me." I got down on my knees and I took that lady's hands and went to prayer, saying, "Lord you're the same God who set *me* free this week. Lord, set *her* free." I want to tell you—the darkness lifted for her, not because of me but because of the faithfulness of our God! That turned into a day of revival in that church!

We fight not against flesh and blood but against the rulers of darkness. There is spiritual warfare going on. I hope you will write two more words into the edge of your Bible: *trial* and *test.* "No temptation [trial or test] has overtaken you except such as is common to man; but God is faithful, who will not allow you to be tempted beyond what you are able, but with the temptation will also make the way of escape, that you may be able to bear it." Praise God! Take courage—don't give up!

So you're going through a hard place? Hold steady! God is not going to allow more than you can bear, and he will provide a way of escape for you! Well, thank the Lord! Share this with others because you know people, and so do I, who need that Scripture promise!

Possibly you need to go to the lake and walk and pray. Remind the Lord that your name isn't Job and you need Satan's heaviness lifted from your heart. Don't you dare quit! Hold steady! God is greater than the temptation, trial, or test! He promised, "I will make a way of escape, that you may be able to bear it!" Believe it today!

5 YOU CAN FAIL WITHOUT BEING A FAILURE: PETER

Matthew 26; John 21:15

I think you've noticed that the last time or two I have been going to the back of my Bible and picking up quotes or phrases I've heard from others. That's where we're going again today: "You can fail without being a failure." Okay, you need to let that one soak in a little.

You can fail without being a failure!

I have an idea somebody wrote that after reading a quote of Thomas Edison, the great inventor in America: "I have not failed—I have just found 10,000 ways that won't work." Then he became *the* inventor of the century—everything from the light bulb to filming and all of that. For 10,000 times he tried items that didn't work as filaments for the light bulb, but don't call him a failure! He failed, but he wasn't a failure.

Do we ever need to hear that one today! I just want to tell you—all of us fail from time to time at something. Of course, I'd like to give you a personal illustration, and I have to say, "Well, shall I tell them this one, or this one, or this one, or that one?"

So back to when I was ten years old, we lived in Boone, Iowa. My mom was a piano teacher. She had forty students, and she must have decided I needed to learn how to play the piano as well. So I had my little piece, and it was ready for the first recital ever—for me. We went down to an auditorium and everybody's parents came, and maybe a few grandmas and grandpas. I was just a little kid, just ten, and I looked at that crowd and something happened in me, and I could tell that I was starting to get all tied up inside.

In a little bit my time came. Mom said, "Jimmy Diehl will now come and play." I got up there, my mind now swirling with all these people watching me. There had to be a thousand people there. (I found out later there were only about a hundred.) But anyway, all of that was working on me and the piano keys all started looking the same. I started in "ta da da"—*that's not right*—and I started getting hotter and said to myself, "Let's try it over." "Do da doe"—*that's not right either.* I was frustrated and Mom got up and said, "Jimmy's okay—he just can't find the note where you start." She came up and played the note—"ding, da, ding." "Try that one" and I think I then played my little piece. I was very embarrassed. I got up and did not sit down on the front seat, where I was supposed to sit after my performance. Instead, I went down the middle aisle, out the back door, into the alley—and vomited. I was sick. I've never touched the piano since!

I failed. I know what caused the failure now that I have looked back on it a few hundred times. It was the fear of a crowd, the fear of people. Well, the Lord had to work on me about five, six, or seven years later. I don't have time to tell you that story, but it's another big story of how God led me to do some things, and now I've stood in front of crowds every Sunday all my adult life. Yes, I failed—but I hope I wasn't a failure.

How about the Bible? I could go from one to the other of men or women who failed, but they gave it to God. They repented, if it was that kind of failure, sinful failure, and they were restored!

I'll just choose one, and that's Peter. He was one of the disciples, the brash one, the self-confident one, the "I've got this under control" one. Jesus was arrested. Peter then kind of followed the crowd and got off at a distance. Jesus was then on trial in the night in front of Caiaphas. Peter was out there in the courtyard, the Bible says, and I reread it just to get it all straight.

A young girl came up to Peter and said, "You were with Him."

'No, I do not know the man."

A second young girl or lady came up: "You belong to Him. I can tell."

"No, no," he said, adding a curse to it.

The third person came up and said, "You *do* belong to Him. I can tell by your accent—you're a Galilean."

Evidently that identified him, and he swore, cursed, and said, "I don't know the man."

Jesus turned around and looked at Peter, and it went through his heart like a dagger. The Bible says, "He went out and wept bitterly."

Peter failed—but he repented. He asked God's forgiveness. I just want you to see in the book of John, at the very end of it, just this paragraph heading: "Jesus Restores Peter." I don't have time to give you all of that, but after the Resurrection Jesus made sure that he went to Peter and restored him.

Peter became the leader of the early church. He became the spokesperson of this movement called Christianity. If you wonder about Peter, why don't you go with me to Rome and see Saint Peter's Basilica? They didn't build all of that for a man who was a failure. The Catholics would say that he was the first pope. Peter was not a failure—he did fail, but he asked for forgiveness because he did a sinful thing. He was restored by Jesus himself.

I just want you to know today that all of us have failed. I went through a whole lot of quotes and felt drawn to that one. Two, three, or a thousand or two may be reading this, and you all need to get this today. You failed, but you don't have to stay down—you don't have to be a failure! Get up! Don't quit! Get up and go again! If you've lost your job, get out, knock on doors, do what you do, search the Internet, go again, don't quit—don't quit!

Peter failed, but he was no failure! Thomas Edison failed, but he was no failure! By the way, Babe Ruth, the great home run king, accomplished seven hundred-plus home runs—and struck out more than a thousand times too! That's failure. You strike out, you sit down on the bench. But don't say Babe Ruth was a failure! He was a champion because when he failed, he said, "Get me back up there. I'm swinging for the fences."

God will help you; God helped me! I know that you need this, or five or ten people you know need it! Share it in some way. We have to tell everybody what I have written down here from the back of my Bible: *You can fail without being a failure!*

Praise God! Thank you, Lord! Pick up your eyes, your heart, your spirit. You're no failure! God has something better for you ahead!

6 I HAVE NO GREATER JOY...

3 John 4

Let me tell you about an experience I had a couple of years ago. It was a Sunday and one busy day for me. I left the house quite early in the morning as my son-in-law, Bernie Gitt, drove me to Denver International Airport. I got onto an airplane and flew to Kansas City. Our son Don and grandson Derek picked me up there. They actually live in Nashville but were in Kansas City.

Then we did what we had to do to be prepared for the three o'clock memorial service for Dr. Paul Cunningham. Now many of you are not connected to the Nazarene world, so you need to know that Paul Cunningham started his ministry in Olathe, Kansas, a few miles southwest of Kansas City, with a Church of the Nazarene running between forty-five and fifty in attendance. He pastored that church thirty years. It eventually grew to three thousand and even more in membership. Then he was elected general superintendent in the Church of the Nazarene (that's the highest elective office we have in our denomination). In that position he traveled around and around the world for sixteen years and then retired.

Dr. Cunningham had recently died and gone to his eternal reward, so we were there with many others for the memorial service.

He was quite well known, of course, so there was a very strong crowd there at the funeral with music that lifted us all the way to heaven.

Then the various speakers came with their prepared short messages. We heard about Dr. Cunningham's accomplishments and about the person he had become. We heard the funny things; we heard the tearful things. Then his three adult children spoke, two daughters and one son. At the finish was shown a video that looked back across the sixty years of ministry of Paul Cunningham.

After the service I was greeting people, shaking hands, and our son Don came and said, "Come on, Dad—we've got fifteen minutes. We have to get you to the airport to get you back home." I was saying "Howdy, howdy," "Good to see you," "God bless you." We jumped into the car, tore off to the airport, I got onto the airplane, and I arrived back in Denver that night, so that was a one-day event for me.

On the flight back I had time to finally calm down and reflect. I got to thinking about the accomplishments of Paul Cunningham, about the tremendous growth as far as attendance and influence of that church. I got to thinking about the honors he had received, and then the part that stood out to me. The highlight of the entire memorial service for me was when his three adult children spoke one by one of their dad. Of course, they told the personal things, the funny things, the cheerful things, the spiritual things, and told how their dad had led them spiritually to Jesus and to the Christ-like life.

My mind went back to my first pastorate, in Muscatine, Iowa—that's fifty-some years ago. In Muscatine I found a fellow who became my friend, and he was excellent in calligraphy. A scripture came to me, and I took it to him and asked, "Can you do that on some kind of a poster?" Here's the scripture: 3 John, verse 4—"I have no greater joy than to hear that my children walk in truth." This was written by the apostle John, who wrote the gospel of John and also 1, 2, and 3

John, as well as the book of Revelation. But when he wrote this, he was an older John; he was an older sage of God, and here he wrote, "I looked back over all of my life; I have no greater joy than to hear that my children walked in the truth."

My friend drew a great piece for me. Then my dad saw this and said, "I want him to do four more because we have five children. I want to get those framed and I want all the Diehl kids to have this on their wall somewhere in the home: "I have no greater joy than to hear that my children walk in truth." That scripture has been hanging on a prominent wall in our home for more than fifty years and will stay on that wall as long as I live.

Dad had that done so that all five of us would have the same thing in our homes all our lives: "I have no greater joy than to hear that my children walk in truth." That's not just a good saying from somewhere—that's the Bible, the Word of God. Today I just want to strongly encourage you that if you have children and they're walking in the truth of Jesus, keep feeding them faith. Give them encouragement, because when you get to the end of the road, I believe you will say, "The greatest joy of my life is that my kids are walking with Jesus."

If you have children and they aren't walking in the truth, I want to strongly say to you today—pray, pray for your kids. Build a bridge—it may take a long time, but build a bridge to your kids, to your sons, to your daughters, to your grandsons, to your granddaughters. Then pray, build the bridge, and then pray. Don't give up on your children. Don't you remember the prodigal son? The father never gave up on that prodigal; he watched and prayed every day. He watched the road—"Is my boy coming back?"—and prayed. You can do that. Build a bridge, pray; don't give up on your kids!

A lot of people who have listened to or read these "Refuels" are single and I hear from many of you. Maybe your children have preceded you in death, or maybe you have no children. I want to encourage you today to adopt some. I'm not talking about that legal thing. I'm talking about adopting a child or a teenager into whom you can pour your life.

I haven't thought of this in years, but this morning as I was trying to refresh my mind, I remembered Elbert Reed of Des Moines, Iowa, my Sunday School teacher when I was twelve or thirteen. He would pick up a couple of his Sunday school boys, take us out once in a while on a Saturday morning for breakfast, talk, just have fun, and be with us. I can remember Elbert Reed saying, "I'm proud of you guys. Serve Jesus, let God have all of you, live your life for the Lord." You see, I was not his son, but he "adopted" me as I wrote about. You could do that too!

If Paul Cunningham could have spoken from his casket, I believe he would have said, "I have no greater joy than to hear that my children walk in truth." May we have the same testimony!

7 FOCUS ON GOD'S FAITHFULNESS, NOT THE FAILURES OF PEOPLE

2 Timothy 4:14, 16–17

Let me tell you a bit about how I go about finding out what to say to you each time. You probably know that "Ten Minutes to Refuel with Pastor Jim Diehl" was a series of YouTube videos that were put out weekly during the COVID-19 pandemic. They have been assembled and are in this book and adapted to this format. But you might wonder how the topics for each video were selected, so I'll explain it here this time.

I've learned to consider everyone who watched as "my church," and we had people "attending" this church from all around the world. This is very encouraging to me with all kinds of different background, cultures, and all. What truth would fit for all of you today? I pray about it, just as I did as a pastor: "Lord, where do you want me to go? What's the next truth you want me to give?"

I was doing that for today and felt led to the back and front of my Bible, where I find all kinds of things written. These are things I've heard from others that I've written down. Then I've used those quotes in preaching.

I felt led to do that for today. I read a whole lot of quotes, finally boiled them down to two, and I have all the notes about that for today. Then this morning as I was reviewing this, it seemed that the Spirit of the Lord was saying, "Just give them one." Two might be a little much, so here it is. From the back of my Bible I found this quote: "Choose to focus on the faithfulness of God rather than the failures of people." Let that soak in a moment: *Choose to focus on the faithfulness of God rather than the failures of people.* I don't know who said that, so I just have "Anonymous" written there—but it's good.

I found a scripture that illustrates this quite well, in the last chapter of 2 Timothy. This was Paul writing to his son in the faith, Timothy. Paul was in his last prison, in his last days before he was to be executed because he was the leader of the Christian movement. So he was not in a happy place, but listen to what he said right at the very end of his letter: "Alexander the coppersmith did me much harm. May the Lord repay him according to his works" (2 Timothy 4:14). In other words, "Alexander really, really did me dirty. Watch out for him, Timothy. Don't let him do that to you, but may the Lord repay him according to his works."

Then he talks about an earlier trial that he had to go through. Read this: "At my first defense no one stood with me, but all forsook me." Those were his friends; those were his buddies; those were his companions—they failed him. It was like when Jesus went on trial—the disciples all forsook him and fled. Look at this from Paul: "At my first offense no one stood with me, but all forsook me. May it not be charged against them" (2 Timothy 4:16).

I want you to see where I'm going here. Paul mentions these failures of friends and the opposition of one named Alexander, but he didn't have the attitude "Alexander the coppersmith did me much harm—I hope his soul burns in hell forever." He didn't say that. He just said, "May the Lord repay him according to his works. I've given him to God. My friends all forsook me and left me. Lord, don't charge it against them."

Let's now read these next words: "But the Lord stood with me and strengthened me, so that the message might be preached fully through me, and that all the Gentiles might hear. Also I was delivered out of the mouth of the lion. And the Lord will deliver me from every evil work and preserve me for His heavenly kingdom. To Him be glory forever and ever. Amen!" (2 Timothy 4:17–18). The man had victory on death row. He did not focus on the failure of friends or others; he focused on the faithfulness of God!

I was in one of my early pastorates. Out in in the lobby area after the Sunday morning service a middle-aged lady blew up, tore into somebody, got to yelling. It was hurtful. There were tears, and people were leaving. I was called to "get out there—so-and-so's chewing somebody apart." After all the singing, all the praying, all the preaching, and everything—then you go home with that.

I just said, "Dear Lord, help us."

Everything was ruined in those five minutes after the service. I waited for two days. On Tuesday I went over to this lady's house. I went in, sat down, and said to her, "There's something in your past that has left you bitter. There's something in your past that's caused you to be angry. What happened Sunday didn't cause that—it's coming from the past. What happened to you?"

She said in a loud voice, "That doctor let my baby die! That doctor let my baby die and I will never forgive him!"

I said, "What?"

She told me all about that hurtful event.

I said, "Wow! When did that happen?"

She said, "Twenty years ago, and I'll never forgive him! That doctor let my baby die and I will never ever forgive him!"

I said, "Dear lady, is there any way we could go to the doctor and resolve this?"

"No, he died. He died ten years ago."

I said, "You mean you have all this bitterness and anger and the man's gone? He's dead? You have to give that to God, lady, or you're going to be miserable all the rest of your life and you're going to cut other people in two. Let it go."

Just as Paul said about Alexander the coppersmith, "I gave him to God. I gave him to God!"

I really felt that today someone, maybe a thousand someones, are reading this, need to give somebody to God. You need to give something to God. You need to give some failure of a friend to God!

I want to repeat it to you one more time: *Choose to focus on the faithfulness of God rather than the failures of people.* Share that with somebody else, because too many people are carrying too much baggage. Let it go. Be set free! Let God come and give you healing! We serve not only a saving God but a healing God as well. Give it to Him!

8 GOD CAN BRING GOOD OUT OF BAD

Philippians 1

The truth I have for today is found in the first chapter of Philippians, and here's the background story. Paul was the leader of the early church. At this point he was the missionary of the early church, the theologian of the church, the church planter of the early church. He was just about everything in leadership. However, he was in prison in a Roman jail for two years and he hadn't done anything wrong except being the leader of the Church of Jesus Christ. It was not popular to be a Christian back in that day! So from a Roman jail for two years we need to click that in—that's not good!

He wrote with whatever he used and wrote these words: "I want you to know, brethren, that the things which happened to me" (he's talking about being in the prison since he talks about his chains in just a moment) "have actually turned out for the furtherance of the gospel, so that it has become evident to the whole palace guard, and to all of the rest, that my chains are in Christ" (Philippians 1:12–13).

What does that mean? I think you have to use your imagination just a little bit while you read the Bible to kind of fill in between the lines. Here's the way I've got it figured out. These Roman guards (Roman soldiers), every single one of them, all watched over Paul at one time or the other. Let's just say two at a time, let's just say they had a day crew and a night crew. I can see two Roman guards walking in at sunrise. I can hear Paul say, "Now, boys, why don't you just sit down over there? I happen to have a chain from my leg down to the floor and I'm not going to get out of here today. But I've been around here long enough that I've got this thing figured out—you're not getting out either until the sun goes down. So sit down. I'm going to tell you about Jesus and how He can set you free."

Well, then, these guards then left at sundown and the midnight crew came in. "Hey, boys—sit down over there. I'm not going to get out of here tonight. You think I'm in chains—but I've been set free. *You're* the guys who are in chains. That's the way I used to be: bound up and living all tied up with all the things the devil had done to me. Let me tell you how Jesus can set you free!" One by one by, another by another, Roman soldiers were becoming Christians, or else his being in prison would not have "furthered the gospel."

Let's translate that to this year, whoever you are and wherever you are. What does that say to us? Well, here's what it says to me: God can bring good out of bad! *God can bring good out of bad!* I'm not going to spend one minute trying to convince you or me or anybody else that it was good for Paul to be in prison. It wasn't. He should have been out doing another missionary journey or helping another church that needed him to help and on and on. It was bad!

But God brought good out of it because Roman soldiers were coming to Jesus! What a lifetime lesson to learn, that God can bring good out of bad! But I believe from what I've learned in life that if we want that to happen, we have to do two things. We have to give it to God and then give God time!" Could I say it again? *We have to give it to God and then give God time!* He doesn't answer every prayer instantaneously and all of a sudden everything is good. No, many,

many times it's a process. God can bring good out of bad, but we have to give it to God—and give Him time!

I think about the COVID-19 pandemic—there was nothing good about it. I'm not going to try to say it was. No, it was not good. In the United States over a million died and in the world several times that number died. That isn't good—it's bad—but God can bring good out of it or any other situation that you're facing or any other burden that's pressing you down or any frustration that you have—if you'll give it to God and then give God time! He can bring good out of it! It's just like Paul in a Roman jail as he started to lead jailers to Jesus.

In one of my early pastorates we were running maybe sixty to seventy in attendance, and a little group of six or seven people kind of decided they were going to tell me as pastor what to do, what not to do, and it became very difficult. It happened to be in a certain Sunday service that right in the middle of the service seven people got up, put their coats on (it was in the wintertime), and walked out the back door of the church. I think they slammed the door, but whether they did or didn't doesn't make any difference, and seven people walked out, never to ever come back.

I thought we had just lost the church. I thought, "We'll never make it now." I think those people probably paid their tithe and "How are we going to make it without that income?" That's a day I can remember forever because that's the day I wanted to fly away. But I had to give them to God!

Now, I'm going to be honest with you. It took more than a one-time prayer for me. It was day after day after day: "Lord, I give them to you. I give them to you! I'm not going to let them ruin me or steal all my joy." I'm sure they had stolen some of it. Could I tell you that in time we had given it to God and tried to get the whole church do the same thing? We had given God time, and the church actually grew to seventy, eighty, ninety, one hundred, one hundred ten, and over about five years grew to an average of one hundred twenty. The Lord taught me a lifetime lesson: *God is greater than seven people.*

Months later, maybe years later, the Lord gave me an insight as to what had happened. The church had been sick. It was as if we had a boil, an infection, and on that day the infection left and the church actually healed and started growing again.

Don't you dare say that Jim Diehl said that if you want your church to grow have to kick seven people out. I didn't say that! I about died because of it, but *God is bigger than seven people!* What's my point? That was bad, it was really bad, but God brought good out of it. The church strengthened, became healthier, and as I said, we had quite a bit of growth.

God bless you today. I want you to believe that truth. God was bigger than a Roman jail; God was bigger than seven people; and God is able to bring good out of bad for you, my friend. Hey, by the way—pass this on to somebody else, share it with somebody who needs it, and I'll pray that it will help them as well. God bless you all.

9 DON'T JUMP OFF A BRIDGE TO RESCUE A HAT

John 5:16

As a young pastor I went to a pastors' conference, along with my wife, Dorothy. A whole bunch of others were there too. A great veteran of the faith, a great preacher and church administrator, was up preaching and said something that I had never heard before. Here's what he said: "Don't jump off a bridge to rescue a hat."

He was talking about a bridge over a river. "Jump off a bridge to rescue a child and you're a hero; jump off a bridge to rescue a hat and you're a fool."

I knew that had to mean something high-powered. So I wrote that down in the back of my Bible along with all the other truths I was learning. That has come back to me over and over across the years: "Don't jump off a bridge to rescue a hat."

What are you talking about? Where is that in the Bible? Well, those words are not in the Bible as such, but the illustration is right here in the gospel of John, chapter five. To make the story very brief, a man who could not walk, a man who had been lame for thirty-eight years, had been coming to the pool of Bethesda. He was waiting there, possibly to be healed by an angel of God who would trouble the waters, but when something would happen, he couldn't get up.

Then Jesus walked by and said to him, "Do you want to be made well?"

The man said, "Yes, but I can't get in the pool."

Jesus looked at the lame man and said, "Rise up, take your bed, and walk!" Instantaneously the man was healed, and he took his bed (which is not a bed like what we use but something like a mat). He headed out. I don't think he walked—I think he jumped. I think he leaped. I think he skipped. After all, the man hadn't walked in thirty-eight years, and he had been healed!

Then what I call the religious police—the Pharisees and some of the other leaders in the Jewish system of that day—got hold of him and said, "Who did this?"

He replied, "I don't know His name," but they found out that it was Jesus. Chapter 5 verse 16: "For this reason the Jews persecuted Jesus, and sought to kill Him, because he had done these things on the Sabbath."

Oh, no! Instead of these religious people, who had forever seen this man, saying, "Wow—you can walk! What happened to you? Congratulations, friend!" it was nothing like that. You would think just common courtesy would say that. "No, no!" they said, "This is the Sabbath. You're not supposed to be carrying your mat!" Therefore, they sought to kill Jesus because He had healed on the wrong day. You talk about jumping off a bridge to rescue a hat; that's about the biggest foolishness you can find. Who cares what day it was? The man was healed by a miracle of God. But it shows again how some people get clear off the track and start majoring on minor things, and there it is! I'd like to say this kind of thing happened just in Bible days, but it's happening in our world and in our churches today.

Lately it's been called the worship wars! What a disgrace! Worship wars! What is that? Are we going to sing the hymns and the gospel songs? Or are we going to sing choruses—some of which are the "7-11" choruses. You've heard this: seven words and you sing those seven words eleven times.

What are we going to do? This issue has started more church fights than I can count: Are we going to keep the choir and let them be part of the worship, or are we going to dismiss the choir and have a praise team? That'll stir up the troops for sure.

Then there is one of the newer ones: Are we going to sit in pews or shall we take the pews out and put in chairs? "God made pews. Pews and church go together." "Yeah, but if we have chairs, we can move them around and have different events happening here." "Oh, bless God—if you take these pews out, I'm going to leave the church."

Well, that's jumping off the bridge for a hat. Why don't we say, "Lord what do *you* think about this?"

You know what I think God would say? "Pews, chairs. Come to Africa with me. Come to India with me. Come to Bangladesh with me—you'll find a church under a tree as people sit on the ground." God doesn't care what you sit on—just go to church! God doesn't care about the style of music—just worship the Lord! Come on now!

This is not the biggest thing that's happened in my life, but in one of the churches that I pastored, the youth always had a Christmas drama and no one wanted to direct the drama that year, so I said I would do it. We had practice on Sunday afternoons. At the very first one I handed out the parts, and then the mother and father of one of the participants came in, and their son went to them. They found out he hadn't gotten the lead in the play but had to be a shepherd. They blew up in the middle aisle of that church, yelling at me and saying all kinds of things like "Our boy never gets the lead!" They walked out and slammed the door shut. They jumped off the bridge for a hat—all over who gets what part in a Christmas drama!

I would like to tell you today that I've never jumped off a bridge for a hat, but the Lord has had to check me more times than I can tell you.

Recently something was bothering me; it was about our structure, and I was actually praying about it. I said, "Lord, what are we going to do about this?"

The Lord said to me in my mind, "I didn't die on the cross for a structure; I died to win people to Jesus." I let the thing go; I had to move on. You know, it's a hard thing to keep "the main thing the main thing," but that's my plea with you today and with me, that we will not focus on the fact that Jesus healed the man on the wrong day. Who cares what day it was? The man was healed by a divine work of God's healing power.

May we refuse to jump off a bridge for a hat. May we live to focus on the main things— not the minor things that don't make an eternal difference anyway. God bless you all.

10 WHEN NOTHING IS HAPPENING —SOMETHING IS HAPPENING

Genesis 50:20

I've been thinking about a couple of the heroes of the Old Testament: Joseph and Daniel. They ended up being heroes, but it sure didn't start that way.

Just briefly, you remember the story of Joseph, sold as a slave by his own brothers. Now, that's about as bad as it gets. He was taken off to godless Egypt and was there under a Pharoah who knew nothing about God or righteous living whatsoever. Because Joseph was such a moral man and believed in Jehovah God, that ended up landing him in prison. Then a freed fellow prisoner who had said he would remember Joseph and get him out of there forgot him, and Joseph was in prison even longer. I want you to remember that he had done nothing wrong—there was no sin and rebellion in his life for which he was being punished. He had done everything right, but there he was, everything out of his control. How many things today are out of our control?

Much the same is Daniel's story. He was also taken captive, transported to Babylon, and it was just as godless as Egypt was to Joseph. There Daniel's strong belief in his Jehovah God, to whom he prayed regularly, landed him in a den of lions. A lion's den! He had done nothing wrong and had done everything right, and yet all the troubles came because he was obedient to God. As with Joseph, everything was out of his control.

The more I think about it, the more applicable that is to our situation. The COVID-19 pandemic was totally out of our control. The ugly divide that is in America, where there is so much anger and bitterness from group to group—it's out of our control. We can't walk somewhere and make a speech and cure what is going on in America—it's genuinely out of our control. Our society has taken God out of the public square, out of our public life until you can hardly display the Ten Commandments in public. These were the solid-rock foundation of America in the beginning. It's out of our control. Go try changing it! You'll see—it's completely out of our control!

But here's the insight that has come to me. Let's go back to Joseph in prison, sold as a slave by his brothers, forgotten. Nothing was happening day by day, day by day—nothing was happening!

But something *was* happening! That's a whole lot like us. It seems as though in many ways nothing good is happening—it seems that it's all bad. However, I just want you to know that while nothing is happening, something *is* happening! God is still in control! To jump to the end of that Joseph story, he was brought out of prison and was put in charge of a major part of the country. He ended up being second in command behind Pharaoh, being the leader of leaders except for Pharaoh. God brought it all together. When nothing was happening, something *was* happening! God was working in the background and brought it out as it should be!

You probably remember how the story ends. The brothers of Joseph ended up having to come to Egypt because that was the only place where there was food due to the terrible famine. Now, Joseph was meeting these very brothers who sold him as a slave. Here's what he said to them—these are classic words found in Genesis 50:19–20—"Do not be afraid. . . . But as for you, you meant evil against me; but God meant it for good." I'd like to make a slight change, just for our understanding: "You meant evil against me, but God turned it into good."

The story I want to tell is certainly not a major story like Joseph's here in the Old Testament or Daniel or any of the others, but I had to look it up in my notes to make sure that I remembered and got it right. It was February 2008, and I had flown all the way to India for a big Nazarene convention. There were four or five hundred people there and it was Thursday, Friday, Saturday, and Sunday. There were three of us folks from America there, and we were all scheduled to speak. Then the big ordination service was Sunday, when we would ordain the new ministers, and of course, that was my responsibility. We were in an extremist part of India and the police chief got hold of the Nazarene leader there and said, "There will be no foreigners speaking in this city and you tell them, or we will take them to jail."

"No, they've come all the way over here."

"No, no, no."

It was a big confrontation and finally the police chief said, "Okay, you can let them speak really early in the morning when nobody is there. But after 9:00 a.m. they had better not be on the platform or I will have the police take them to jail."

There I was. I was supposed to speak every day.

"But you can't. What are we going to do about the ordination? What are we going to do about the Bible college graduation? They're all here. What are we going to do? All of us who are involved in these events can't even talk because we were forbidden to speak."

While nothing was happening—something *was* happening. Thursday, Friday, and Saturday went by. Saturday night the police came to our leader and said, "You've cooperated. We appreciate it.

Those foreigners have not been speaking past the nine o'clock hour. We're not coming tomorrow. You can do what you want to do. We're not even going to come. Do as you like!"

Our people came and said, "We're free tomorrow. We can have graduation! We can have the ordination. You can preach as long as you want!" The place was packed full on Sunday morning. We had the graduation—caps, gowns, and everything. Another person from our church headquarters in Kansas City spoke to them. Then the ordination service. I ordained twenty-one new pastors one by one. We were singing; the people were blessed. I had in my notes that we didn't get out of there until 1:30 p.m. It was worth the trip!

What's my point? While nothing was happening, something *was* happening. God was working behind the scenes and God did it! I was there! I heard the police chief. I heard the anger and the determination. God worked that around until the chief said, "Do what you want."

I want you to know without a doubt—when nothing is happening, something *is* happening! God is at work. *Don't give up!*

11 PRAY, COMMIT, TRUST, WAIT

Psalm 37:5, 7; 39:12

My last thoughts were about "When nothing is happening, something is happening." I heard from various people about that, but I had the feeling that I didn't quite finish, that I needed to explain one more part of that. The next day I received an email from wonderful songwriter and gospel singer Mark Murphy, from Selma, Indiana. He watched that video and decided to write the following song:

Joseph, Joseph of old—
The Bible told
How his brothers' plans were bad.
As a slave he was sold;
To Egypt he would go,
And that was the end of that.
What they didn't know was God's in control
To bring good from their bad.

When nothing is happening,
Something is happening,
And that's a matter of fact!

CHORUS:
When nothing is happening,
Something is happening.
I can promise you:
When nothing is happening,
Something is happening.
God's gonna see you through.

So don't give up.
Keep looking up.
I can promise you . . .
When nothing is happening,
Something is happening!
God's gonna see you through!
(Used by permission)

I think that's great. Then he has a second verse that goes on about Daniel, which I think you'll like. We'll hear that being sung someday on gospel radio.

Back to Joseph, who was sold by his brothers into slavery—they took him to Egypt, where he was purchased as a slave by Potiphar, a man of leadership and much authority. He took Joseph to his house. Long story made really short, Potiphar's wife took a liking to Joseph and laid a trap for him to get him to go lie with her. When she finally confronted him and grabbed him, the Bible says, she said, "Come lie with me"—and Joseph took off running. That's the most courageous thing he did up to that point in his life. He left his jacket with her and got out of the place. When Potiphar came home later, his wife lied about Joseph and said, "He came in here to sexually assault me. Here's his coat as proof." Potiphar became very angry, got hold of Joseph, and threw him into prison. It was a frame-up, all a lie.

Joseph, a man of God, a spiritual, godly young man, was in now prison for not doing anything wrong and everything right. The Bible says in Genesis 41:1, "At the end of two full years"—that's a long time to be in prison. It's a long time for having done nothing wrong. Two full years. I don't have anything in my life that really coincides with that directly because I have never been sent to prison. I've been to prison in order to visit, but not as an inmate.

Despite this, I have indeed had a two-year dark road, a hurtful, impossible road. That's when our youngest son, Dave, took sick by way of melanoma cancer. We lived not far apart, and I watched our boy die. That's the hardest prison I've ever been in, if you understand what I'm saying.

So "when nothing is happening, something is happening." My mind went back to what Joseph did for two years to stay in tune with God. It doesn't really say in the Bible what he did, but I know what *I* did.

Number one: *pray* when you're in a situation you can't solve, in a situation in which nothing good is happening. Pray! Let me go to the scripture and allow the psalmist to answer all of these: "Hear my prayer, O Lord, and give ear to my cry; Do not be silent at my tears" (Psalm 39:12). *I'm praying to you, Lord; I'm weeping. I cannot fix this; hear my prayer.* I want you to know that I think it's proper to pray every day, several times, about your day, about your prison, about your impossibility. *Lord, I'm still trusting you.*

Number two: *commit* it to Christ! The psalmist said in Psalm 37:5, "Commit your way to the Lord, trust also in Him, and He shall bring it to pass." Commit it to the Lord. I know there are at least two schools of thought at this point. Once you commit it, it is there—leave it! That's one school of thought. The other is to commit it every day. That happens to be my school of thought. God doesn't need to have you go through it over and over again. Maybe I'm just reminding myself that *I've got it committed to you, Lord.* Pray and commit!

Number three: *trust!* Trust the Lord. It says right here, "Commit your way to the Lord, trust also in Him" (Psalm 37:5). This is so good from Corrie ten Boom: "When a train goes through a tunnel and it gets dark, you don't throw away the ticket and jump off the train. You sit still and trust the engineer." Oh, that is good! When you're going through a tunnel and it gets dark, sit still. Don't throw away your ticket and give up on God—just trust the engineer!

Number four: you *wait!* "Rest in the Lord, and wait patiently for him" (Psalm 37:7). No, no, no—that's not easy, but we wait!

That's the outline I lived by for two years: *pray, commit, trust, wait!* I still live by that. What happened to Dave? God answered prayer, but differently than I wanted. God took Dave home to heaven, but he gave me a promise, and with this I'll have to close. As I was watching him take his last breath in that hospital in Colorado Springs and then he died, the Lord whispered in my ear, "Dave didn't die—he just changed his address from Colorado Springs to heaven. He is still alive and there's no more cancer."

Well, praise God! Remember: *pray, commit, trust, wait!* God bless you! Somebody you know needs to read this. Share this with him or her! We're all together in this thing, and if we can help each other, let's do it—and don't give up. "When nothing is happening, something is *going* to happen" and God's going to see you through it! Bless you all!

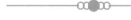

12 GOD OPENS THE BIG GATE. WE OPEN THE LITTLE GATE.

Acts 12

Previously I was in Acts 12 telling the story about Peter, the leader of the early church. I talked about how Herod, the wicked king, had him arrested and put into prison. Peter was to be brought out for his execution on a given day. The night before that, there was an all-night prayer meeting going on at Mary's home, whose son was named John Mark. (He was the one who ended up writing the gospel of Mark.) In the middle of the night God moved by sending an angel to the prison. The angel awakened Peter, the chains fell off his wrists, and the angel walked him out of the prison through guard gates one and two. The iron gates opened of their own accord, according to the scripture, and Peter was set free. Then the angel disappeared, and Peter headed toward Mary's home, where the prayer meeting was being held.

He came to the little gate in front of Mary's house and knocked on the gate. According to the Bible, they were praying inside, probably making some noise for sure, and finally a young teenager—we believe it was a young lady named Rhoda—heard somebody knocking at the gate. She went to the gate and instead of opening it, she heard Peter greet her and ran back into the house exclaiming, "Peter's at the gate! Peter's here!"

I can hear them say," No, no, Rhoda. He's destined to die—he's in prison."

She insisted, "He's at the gate!" They finally ran through the house, went to the gate, and opened it—and there was Peter! He recounted what had happened to him, and if I could just put it in our USA English, "I'm going to die someday, but I'm not dying by Herod's wicked hand when the sun comes up. Blessed be the name of the Lord!"

What's the truth for us from that? God opened the big iron gate and got him out of prison in the middle of the night because only God could. Well, the question came to me: If God got him out of "the big house" through the big prison gate, why didn't God open the *little* gate and let the man into the house? The answer is—there were probably around fifty people, give or take a few, in the house. They could easily open the little gate, and therein is a truth that I've lived by for years: God can open the impossible gates—we're responsible to open the little gates of obedience on our part. How true it is!

You remember when Jesus resurrected Lazarus, who had been dead four days. That was a miracle of God! Then do you know what the Bible says when Lazarus came forth and stood there? Jesus said to Mary and Martha, "Loose him and let him go." They had to undo all the burial clothing and turn the man loose. God did His part—Mary and Martha had to do their part.

Now I need to give you a story that I trust will illustrate this. I was called to be the pastor of Denver First Church of the Nazarene. I had agreed to start on the first Sunday of May. I found out that the church had an extremely heavy obligation of $131,000 that was to be paid by the end of May, which is a tremendous amount of money. Some were saying, "Let's just borrow the money and pay it back later. It's too much to hit you with at the beginning." Others were saying, "Let's just forget it and maybe some other day we can address the problem."

Either way, I went to prayer. Now, I hadn't officially become the pastor. That was coming on Sunday. I was moaning and groaning, saying, "Lord, what are we supposed to do? What are we supposed to do?"

I felt clearly that the Lord impressed on my mind and my heart, "You serve them for one month at no pay, no income—tell the people you will sacrifice that. Ask the people to sacrifice and see what I will do for you." I got up that Sunday and I told them that exact thing. I said, "I haven't told a living soul because I don't want anybody talking me out of it. I'm going to serve for a month, no pay whatsoever. What sacrifice will *you* make?"

After the service I was shaking hands with the people and a little older lady came up to me. Her name was Bernice Bedan. She fumbled around in her purse, pulled out her Social Security check, handed it to me, and said, "Here, Pastor. I feel like God wants me to give all of this to help meet this need."

I said, "No, no, no, no. I can't take that. That's your check for the month."

The words she said stopped me cold: *"How come you can mind God and I can't?"*

"Oh, no!" I took that check. I put my arm around that little lady. I know I welled up with tears, and you know what I said the next Sunday morning: "Look at this check, folks. Bernie Bedan gave her whole month's check. That's sacrifice. What are *you* going to do?"

Well, it got down to the last Sunday of the month and the last service Sunday night. We were $3,000 short, and that's a miracle in itself. But I got up and told the people, "We've got to all dump in a little bit more. Is there any anything left in your billfold or your purse or your checkbook?" We received the offering, went on with the service, I stood up to preach, and our financial director, Dave Brown, walked down the aisle and came right up onto the platform. I was already up there starting to preach. He handed me a piece of paper. We had gone over the top by $3,000—a total of $134,000! "We made it! We made it! We made it!" It was an impossible need, but we made it with the help of God. I announced it, and people jumped up on their feet, started clapping, some crying, some waving their hands in the air.

Our worship leader, Michael Cork, came up and said, "We need to sing." We started singing, and to my memory I never preached a message that night. It was "hallelujah time"!

What's my point? I believe that was a miracle of God, but I had to open the little gate of obedience and serve one month with no income. Bernice Bedan gave her whole Social Security check; that's opening the little gate. God did the big thing, and an entire congregation did their part.

What do you need to do to see the real answer to prayer? Do you need to apologize to somebody about something? Do you need to make a phone call and start building a bridge? Do you need to maybe pay a debt that you're irritated about? Whatever it is, you just need to do it. What little gate is there that you need to open to allow God to open the big iron gate?

My friend, that's the point for today. God will do the impossible, but we have to open the little gate. Will you do that? I don't know who you are, but God will honor you, and there will be a miracle in the making! Thank the Lord, the big gates are for God; the little gates are for us! Together with God = miracles!

13 IT BOILS DOWN TO TWO THINGS

Matthew 22:34–40

I'm writing this in September, and this past Saturday was my birthday. I don't make a big deal out of that, but I received many greetings. Of course, many were via Facebook, email, Messenger, texting, telephone calls, plus letters and cards that came through the mail. It was very heartwarming to hear from various corners around the world, as well as across the US. I think I heard from people from about every chapter of my life.

I started thinking, *You know, I'm not to the end of the journey yet. I think I've got ten years yet to go; only God knows. But I'm older than I used to be. What's really worth it in life? What's worth the investment in my life?* What's worth the investment in *your* life?

Some of you have heard me preach and have heard me say this, but it fits in again right now. I have come to believe that we ought to do two things with our one life. Number one: *Get totally right with God.* Number two: *Invest your life in people.* I believe it now more than ever.

First, get totally right with God. Now, I don't have time to amplify this much in this space we have, but let me just say this: there's a whole lot more to the Christian life than asking forgiveness and being born again. Thank God for that and what a miracle is the new birth in our lives. But this Christian life is a whole lot like being married—there's a whole lot more to marriage than the wedding! I really want you to get that now—there's a whole lot more to marriage than the wedding. Yes, of course you need a wedding. All of that—and more—makes a marriage. But there's a life to be lived, there are joys, there are sorrows, there are mountain peaks, there are valleys, there's a life to be lived, and yes, you need a wedding, but that's not marriage.

You also need to be born again and so do I! But somewhere along your spiritual journey the Holy Spirit is going to bring this to you as a challenge: "You have given me your sins—now give me *yourself!*" That's a different prayer. That's a prayer of consecration, a prayer of "I surrender myself to God"! That's a deeper prayer of "Yes, Lord. You can have *all* of me." It's more than saying, "Forgive me, Lord"! Get totally right with God—don't stay back in kindergarten spiritually. Get growing!

Second, invest your life in people. If you would invest your life in money, in values, or in all the education in the world—which I'm not against, and neither am I against money—if you invest your life in properties, houses, and land, every bit of that you're going to leave behind when life is over. You're going to leave it! But if you invest your life in *people,* they will live forever, either in God's heaven or in the devil's hell. People are eternal souls. Invest your life in *people*!

Jesus said it a whole lot better than I can say it. Here is it in Matthew: "Then one of them, a lawyer, asked Him a question, testing Him, and saying, 'Teacher, which is the great commandment in the law?' Jesus said to him, '"You shall love the Lord your God with all your heart, with all your soul, and with all your mind." This is the first and great commandment. And the second is like it: "You shall love your neighbor as yourself"'" (Matthew 22:35–39). Now, isn't that something? Get totally right with God, love God with all your heart, all your mind, all your soul, and all your strength—and then invest your life in people. Love your neighbor!

I want you to know that some people, a lot of people, have invested in me. They have helped. Way back when I was in high school in my junior year, I gave my heart to the Lord and was born again. Then came my senior year of high school, and by then I had to settle the matter of God wanting me to be a preacher. So for my high school graduation—I want you to get this now— my pastor at First Church of the Nazarene in Des Moines, Iowa, gave me a copy of *Cruden's Concordance,* which you can use to find virtually any scripture in the Bible for which you're looking. Inside he wrote, "To James Harvey Diehl, High School Graduation, From Your Pastor, C. E. Stanley," and wrote a scripture there. I used this book even this week, and that is just a symbol of his investment in me.

Oh, I have more stories of people investing in me, but I can't give you everything here today. I want you to know that you can do that for others. You can invest in them, you can be a mentor to them, you can be an encourager to them.

As I was getting this thought put together this morning, the Holy Spirit whispered to me, *The greatest need today when you invest in people is to become an encourager . . . an encourager!* As I write this chapter, I have in my hands the birthday cards that came last week. Why do I have them as I am doing this "Refuel"? Because people encourage me by what they say, plus those who have sent messages to me by email, phone calls, Messenger, text, or Facebook: they are encouraging me.

You can be an encourager!! You don't have to have a college degree to be an encourager; you just have to have a heart that loves God and loves people! Today I feel that's what the Lord wants me to tell you. Most important of all, get totally right with God, and then invest your life in people! With all we've got going in this world, people need an encouraging word!

By the way, I always title these brief messages, and as you can see above, the title of this one is "It Boils Down to Two Things." Those two things are—get totally right with God and invest your life in people. Do it today. You can make an eternal difference in someone's life!

14 LIVING IN JOY

Luke 24:31–32, 52–53

As I write this chapter, the Sunday coming up is Palm Sunday and the Sunday following is Easter. One of the components of the Easter story is joy! Can you imagine the joy that was there when Mary Magdalene and the other Mary left that empty tomb and ran to the disciples and shouted, "The tomb is empty! Jesus is alive!" Come, come, come, come—that was joy! Hilarious joy!

Can you imagine that Easter afternoon on the road to Emmaus? Two men were walking, and all of a sudden the resurrected Jesus joined them, but they didn't know it was Jesus! They talked and talked and finally got to where they were going. They invited this stranger to join them for a meal. While they were eating, Jesus opened their eyes so they could really see and understand. Then they saw that it *was* Jesus! He then disappeared from their sight, so they ran all the way back to Jerusalem and found the disciples and said, "We've seen Jesus! Jesus is alive!"

I love the way the Scripture talks about those two believers: "Then their eyes were opened, and they knew Him; and He vanished from their sight. And they said one to another, 'Did not our heart burn within us while He talked with us on the road and while He opened to Scriptures to us?'" (Luke 24:32). Their hearts were burning within them. That's not sorrow—that's pure joy!

Now it was Easter evening, the first day of the week, and Jesus had been resurrected that morning. The disciples were in a room behind locked doors, and all of a sudden Jesus was there and appeared before them! The Bible says that at first they were terrified. Wouldn't you be as well? They thought maybe they were seeing a ghost, but then that fear turned into joy! *Jesus is alive! Jesus is alive!* Joy unspeakable!

Holy Week starts with the crowd of people crying out, "Hosanna! Hosanna! Jesus is the son of David, the King of the Jews!" Holy Week closes with the resurrection and the overwhelming joy when the followers of Jesus learned His body had not been stolen—He had been resurrected! Powerful joy!

Here's my word to you today: Jesus wants you, Christian friend, to be filled with joy! Remember in the book of Galatians the fruit of the Spirit is listed: love, joy, peace, long-suffering, kindness, goodness, faithfulness, gentleness, and self-control. Please hear me—the devil is trying to steal the joy from every Christian's heart! He's also trying to steal the joy from our worship services. I realize we've come through a pandemic in the last few years and God knows there hasn't been much joy in that, but I believe it's time to reclaim the joy. I'm not talking about being "happy, happy, happy." I'm talking about deep *joy* that comes from the Holy Spirit.

During my tenure of sixteen years as a general superintendent in the Church of the Nazarene, I had to make a hard decision with which not everyone agreed. That's part of the price of leadership. Some months later a man from an unnamed state wrote me a scathing letter from which I'll quote a few lines. "You are corrupt. You are evil. You will stand at the judgment, and you will be condemned to hell. You are truly a rotten man." The letter gets worse but that's enough for now. To be very honest, that didn't bring me joy! Did Satan ever play that over and over in my mind!

I prayed about it. I prayed some more about it. I finally had to do what the old-time preachers would proclaim: "Give it to God. Put it on the altar. Give the man to God and let God deal with him." I finally came to that very decision, committed the person to God, and left him there on the altar of God. Please believe me—God restored my joy! Satan tried to steal it, but God restored the deep joy in my soul. I'm sure you can relate to this true story with one from your life.

Christian friend, let's reclaim the joy! Let's reclaim the joy of the Lord! Luke closes his gospel by writing, "And they worshipped him, and returned to Jerusalem with great joy, and were continually in the temple praising and blessing God" (Luke 24:52–53). Amen! They had great joy; they couldn't keep quiet. Lord, may we reclaim the joy!

Don't let your joy be dependent on what he said, what she did, what they did! Let's rejoice in Jesus Christ as the King, the Lord, the risen Savior!

You may need to put on the altar of God some people who wounded you, so let me encourage you—*do it today!* You can't change what they did or said, but you can commit them to Christ. Our Lord will heal your heart and restore your joy! *Do it today!*

15 LIVING IN PEACE

John 20:19–21, 26; 14:27

This is Easter week, "Holy Week," as we call it in the Christian world. What a special week it is! In the last Refuel I spoke to you about the component of Easter, which is joy. Joy started on Palm Sunday with "Hosannas," and then on Easter morning the joy of Jesus being alive! Now it is Easter evening. Jesus had been resurrected but the disciples had not seen Him yet. He had been seen by Mary and Mary Magdalene and others, including the two men on the road to Emmaus. It was now evening and the disciples were in a room behind locked doors, still filled with fear.

"The same day at evening, being the first day of the week, when the doors were shut where the disciples were assembled, for fear of the Jews, Jesus came and stood in the midst, and said to them, 'Peace be with you'" (John 20:19). They were startled and frightened, thinking they had seen a ghost, so Jesus added, "Peace to you! As the father has sent Me, I also send you!" (v. 21). He's alive! He's alive! Jesus is alive! The joy that must have come into that room of the disciples! Believe it—*Jesus is alive.*

But one disciple was not there, Thomas. He missed all of this first meeting with the resurrected Jesus. Now it is eight days later, and the disciples are back in a room and Thomas is with them. "Jesus came, the doors being shut, and stood in the midst, and said, 'Peace to you!' Then He said to Thomas, 'Reach your finger here, and look at My hands; and reach your hand here, and put it into My side. Do not be unbelieving, but believing'" (vv. 26–27)—because Thomas had said, "Unless I can see the print in His hands and the piercing in His side, I will not believe" (that's why he has been known as "doubting Thomas").

Jesus said *peace* to them repeatedly. That was not a coincidence. It was not like Jesus saying, "Hey, fellas—how are you doing?" He was trying to communicate a huge truth to them—"Peace I give to you!"

Now let's go back a week or ten days when Jesus was having his last talks with his disciples before the crucifixion. "Peace I leave with you, My peace I give to you; not as the world gives do I give to you. Let not your heart be troubled, neither let it be afraid" (John 14:27).

Peace I leave with you! My peace I give to you! You've caught it by now. In the last Refuel we saw great joy. This time we're focusing on *peace!* Jesus said it several times, and now we've picked up what He had promised just before the agony of Holy Week: "Peace I give to you!" Well, my friend, I want to tell you what you already know: there *isn't* any peace in the world! Hatred, crime, and deception are everywhere. There is no peace!

But one of Jesus's titles is "the Prince of Peace." When we receive Jesus into our hearts, we receive His peace! If we as persons or as a nation reject Jesus, we're rejecting peace! No wonder there's no peace around. Jesus has been blocked out, and therefore peace is gone. Warren Wiersbe, a true scholar, author, and speaker, wrote, "Life is full of disturbances; without and within are fears—there is no peace! A dozen open doors beckon to us for some kind of peace—escape, entertainment, alcohol, sex, drugs, and hard work. We run from one door to the other hoping to find peace. What we need is Jesus Christ, for his name is 'Prince of Peace,' and that takes care of the agonies of life!" What a great statement!

I want you to know I've gone through my share of darkness, agony, sorrow, and death. Our forty-five-year-old son died of melanoma cancer, and I understand grief. Here's what I had to do: I had to quit asking why because far too many questions of life have no answers. I had to give Dave's death to God and in my soul. I don't know who all I'm writing to today, but the devil is trying to steal your peace. Quit asking why he, she, they—why did they do that? You'll never get all the answers. Surrender it to God and let the Prince of Peace, Jesus the Resurrected One, bring you true peace!

Yes, Satan is trying to steal your peace, but God is greater! Our God is a healing God. Give your wounded heart to Him and leave it there. Jesus, the Prince of Peace, will slowly but surely heal your heart and restore your peace. I know—I've been there! God is greater!

16 ANGEL IN DISGUISE

Psalm 91:11

This week I feel led to look into the general theme of heaven. Normally we think of angels as residing in heaven—that's their home—although they're out and about doing the work of God. Well, I've had two experiences in my life that I really believe were "angel encounters," and I'm going to tell you one today.

It was August 18, 1984, and I was living in Hastings, Nebraska. I was invited by four or five churches in the Canyon City area of Colorado to come out that summer in August to hold an outdoor camp-meeting-type crusade. For four or five nights we went to a rodeo grounds and the people sat in the stands. A flatbed truck served as our platform. After the Friday night service, two pastors and their spouses came up to me and said, "Hey—we'd like to go whitewater rafting tomorrow on the Arkansas River, which is right near here. Would you like to go with us?"

I said, "Sure. I've always wanted to go whitewater rafting, but we don't have whitewater much in Nebraska or even Iowa, from where I came originally." So they told me to be ready mid-morning on Saturday. They came by the motel, and I got into the car with Gene and Nola Haynes, one of the pastors there, and Dale Dieter and his wife,

Sharon, another pastor in the Canyon City area. The Dieters had a ten-year-old son named Brian, who also came along.

I need to tell you some things I did not know about whitewater rafting. First of all, I did not know that there had been monsoon-type rains in the mountains and that the Arkansas River was at virtually snow-melt level. I didn't know that Gene and Nola had just the week before purchased the rubber raft that was on top of the car with ropes down through the windows that they were holding onto. This was going to be this raft's maiden voyage down the river. I didn't know that to go whitewater rafting you need a full upper-body life vest and a helmet. I didn't know that the professionals use long oars to keep those rafts going the right way—but we had only short, stubby little oars. We got in the car and started up Highway 50 ascending the mountain adjacent to the river. We eventually found the place that they had searched out ahead of time.

We got out, took the raft off the car, went down to the river, and prepared to launch. Everybody was laughing, having a good time. Then I found out that this was the first time they had ever gone whitewater rafting—also my first time, of course. They all got into the raft, and I told them I would push them into the river and then jump in. I could clearly remember my last words: "We're either going to have the time of our lives or we're all going to make the *Herald of Holiness*." That was our Nazarene denominational magazine—I was thinking about the obituary section.

I pushed them out, jumped into the raft, and the turbulent river immediately started turning that raft around in circles. I knew that wasn't right, and last thing I heard was Nola's little oar slapping the water and Gene yelling, "Row, Nola, row! Row, Nola, row!" The rubber raft hit one of the boulders in the river, capsized, and six of us were thrown into the raging river.

I started tumbling in the water and hitting the rocks. My hat was long gone from the power of the river, and the violent current ripped off my tennis shoes from back to front. I knew that when I came up for air I needed to gasp air and that when I was under the water I had better shut my mouth and not swallow the water or I would be dead. As I came up I saw on the highway that ran adjacent to the river a lady running the way I was tumbling. I noticed she was dressed in red slacks and some kind of a red-and-white shirt. I was being swept down the river rolling and tumbling. The lady was still with me, running on the highway, keeping up with me.

According to a professional who was behind us trying to catch up to help us, I was in the river from ten to twelve minutes. I should have died! I should have drowned! But I finally was thrown onto a rock. I put a death grip on that rock, wheezing and spitting. I couldn't talk since I had swallowed so much water. The lady in red worked her way down the embankment and yelled something at me. I couldn't talk—I couldn't let loose of the rock. She plunged into the river, came to me, and grabbed me. I put a death grip on her as she drug me to the bank. By then some men had come down from the highway to help, got hold of me, and said, "We have to get you up to the highway." One got on one side and one on the other. I said, "Wait a minute—where's the lady?"

They said, "What lady?"

I said, "Some lady dressed in red pulled me off that rock out there. I didn't come in here myself. I was out on that rock."

"Oh, we didn't see any lady."

We got up to the highway and soon the others were coming, wet and looking drowned, and we were hugging each other, crying, and laughing. Then Brian's mom cried out, "Where's Brian? Where's Brian?"

In a moment Brian came running down the highway from upstream and came hugging on his mom and his dad and the rest of us. Then we hugged each other. Brian said to Nola, the other pastor's wife, "Nola, when we flipped over my feet got caught in that rope that goes around the raft, and you undid my feet and shoved me to the shore."

She said, "No, Brian—I didn't see you. I was thrown toward the bank."

He said, "Some woman undid my feet and shoved me to the shore." I looked at him and wondered, *Was she dressed in red?* I've thought about that a thousand times since then, probably ten thousand times, and there's not a doubt in my mind that she was an angel of God. I am just as sure that she also undid Brian from the rope, then ran down the highway to rescue me and disappeared.

A few years later I was called to Colorado to live, serve, and minister there. I went back down to the river one day and found where we were pulled out. I went down, stood by the river, looked, and prayed and thanked God. I should have drowned! I then saw a big stick in the river locked in between some rocks. I pulled the stick out of the river and I have it in my office to this day. It is a symbol that says, "He shall give His angels charge over you, to keep you in all your ways. In their hands they shall bear you up, Lest you dash your foot against a stone." That, of course, comes from Psalm 91 (vv. 11–12). I should have died! God sent an angel—and I'm alive!

If you don't believe this story, I won't worry about it. I was there. I was in the river ten to twelve minutes. *I should have drowned.* God sent a lady, an angel dressed in red. When I get to heaven I'm going to ask to meet that angel. I want to hug her one more time and say, "Thank you." She was an angel in disguise on August 18, 1984. I am still rejoicing today!

17 JESUS SAVED MY SOUL

Acts 9:1–6

Last time I was talking about how an angel of God saved my life out of the tempestuous Arkansas River. After I finished the angel story, I started praying, "Okay, Lord—where do we go next?" Here's what came to me: *An angel saved my life, but Jesus saved my soul.* That's a bigger miracle than being saved out of a river, but it's not quite as dramatic.

First of all, let me tell you about a man named Saul in the New Testament. Saul of Tarsus was a young man full of zeal, energy, and determination. All of that is good *except* that he was going the wrong way. He hated Christians and was out to persecute them. In chapter 9 of Acts Saul was "breathing threats and murder against the disciples of the Lord" (v. 1). He went to the high priest and asked permission to go to Damascus to arrest any and every Christian he could find. He planned to bring them back into court, either to be jailed or killed, because that is what they were doing in those days. He was on his way to Damascus on the Damascus Road, and "suddenly a light shone around him from heaven. Then he fell to the ground, and heard a voice saying to him, 'Saul, Saul, why are you persecuting Me?'

"And he said, 'Who are You, Lord?'

"Then the Lord said, 'I am Jesus, whom you are persecuting'" (vv. 3–5).

Then Saul said as he was "trembling and astonished, 'Lord, what do You want me to do?'" (v. 6). The light must have been brilliant because any light around Jesus or God the Father is nothing less than unbelievably brilliant. It knocked him to the ground, and this chapter of Acts tells how his conversion took place.

My story does not hold a candle to Saul's. As you might know, Saul became Paul and wrote much of the New Testament, becoming the leader of the band called Christians. Back to me now. What's *my* story? I was just coming into my junior year in high school and was sixteen. I was raised in the church. Mom and Dad were solid-rock Christians, but my problem was that I was living on Mom and Dad's religion. They were Christians for sure—we prayed at home, we prayed over meals, we went to church quite a bit. Sure, I was a "Christian"—but in truth I was riding on Mom and Dad's religion. There are a lot of people like that!

My brother Rich was four years younger. Rich and I had our bedroom upstairs in a screened-in back porch. That's where we were in the spring, summer, and fall. In the winter we would go down to the basement where we had a place all laid out for our bedroom. We had bunk beds; Rich was up above and I was down below.

God must have said, "It's time to knock Jim Diehl off his horse." It's not as dramatic as Saul's experience, but here's what happened. I was in bed; I could hear outside noises because the room was screened in. We were only a block away from Harding Road, which was the main road to Broadlawns General Hospital, and Broadlawns was where they would take accident victims. It was about midnight and I heard a siren. I could tell it was an ambulance siren, not a fire truck or a police car, and I heard that thing go by a block away –"Yeowww." You don't even think about it when you hear sirens a lot, but from another part of town I heard another siren, and it was working its way to Harding Road—"Yeowww." So help me—then *another* siren from another part of town started screaming.

All of a sudden all the preaching I had ever heard about the rapture came to me, about Jesus coming back as in the scripture that says two will be in bed and one will be taken, the other left; two will be working in the field and one will be taken, the other left, and so on. When Christ comes in the rapture, the Christians will be carried away, and I had heard preaching on that for sixteen years. I thought, *Oh, no! Oh, no! The rapture has happened! Jesus has come! Cars are wrecking everywhere! Christians are being taken away from their cars and their cars are going crazy. Oh, Lord, help us! Lord, help us!* I'll admit God used those sirens to awaken this pretty self-sufficient teenager!

I got out of bed and honestly, I looked up to see if Rich was there, and he was sound asleep. I said, "That doesn't do me any good. Rich isn't living any better than I am." (Forgive me, Rich. He got right with God later.)

I walked down the hall and down the stairs of our home thinking, *If Mom and Dad are here, I've got a chance! If Mom and Dad are gone, I'm dead meat!* I walked into Mom and Dad's bedroom and there they were! I thought, *Oh, thank you, Jesus. The rapture hasn't come! I've got a chance!*

Mom was not a sound sleeper, and she awakened and said, "Jim, what's the matter with you?"

I just blurted it out, "Mom, I thought the rapture had come and I'm not ready, and I knew if you and Dad were here, I've still got a chance!"

Mom said, "Why don't you get right with God now and you won't have anything to worry about?"

I said, "I'm ready!"

She elbowed Dad and said, "Dad, wake up. Jim wants to pray!"

He got down on one side of me, Mom on the other side, and they started praying for me. I asked God to forgive me for all my selfish ways and what I wanted to do in life and all my sins. Somewhere about 12:30 a.m. I was born again! I was forgiven. I was saved at the bedside of Dad and Mom! They hugged me, and we all cried. I said something like "Thank you, God! Thank you, Mom and Dad!"

I headed back upstairs. Now, I'm not making this up—I got into my bed, I pulled those covers up, and I said out loud, "Come on back, Jesus! I'm ready now!" I went to sleep with peace. An angel saved my life out of the Arkansas River—but Jesus saved my soul! That's a bigger miracle. It's not quite as flamboyant a story, but it's a powerful miracle because it lasts forever!

I've got more to my story because that's just the beginning, when I was born again like a new baby. There's a whole lot more to it than that! But you have to be born again before you can grow in Christ Jesus. I'm about to run out of space, so let me ask you: *Have you been born again? Have you been forgiven? Does Christ live in your heart?* Don't live on your mom and dad's religion! Don't live on your husband's or wife's religion! You have to have Jesus in your own heart!

Share this with others. It will either reinforce what they believe, or it may be used by God as He used three ambulances to awaken this self-sufficient teenager. I'm ready now—come, Lord Jesus! I wish He would! May you be ready! Amen, and again—amen!

18 THERE'S MORE TO THE CHRISTIAN LIFE THAN FORGIVENESS

Romans 12:1

A couple of chapters back I was telling you the story of an angel who saved my life from a turbulent Arkansas River. Then I went over to something more miraculous, as far as I'm concerned—that Jesus saved my soul! That angel saved my life, but Jesus saved my soul! I feel compelled to go on one more step with my story—I want you to know there's more to the Christian life than forgiveness. That's the beginning, but that's not the end! There's more to it than graduating from kindergarten.

Here's what happened, and I'll try to make it as condensed as possible. I was a junior in high school, if you remember, and attended First Church of the Nazarene in Des Moines, Iowa. After I really, really got right with God at the bedside of Mom and Dad in the middle of the night, in the next short period something happened to many of us teenagers of that church. We decided to get off the back pews and go down to the front and get serious about serving Jesus. The youth of Des Moines First Church took the center section, row one, row two, and possibly row three. I'm now down front, carrying my Bible to church and taking notes of what the pastor was saying (fact is, he wanted me to tell him after the service what he said). As I was there listening to the pastor, I heard this whisper, the still small voice of the Holy Spirit: *I want you to be a preacher.*

"No, no, no!"

Nobody had whispered—that was the whisper of the Holy Spirit in my mind and heart.

I want you to be a preacher.

"No, no, Lord. I don't want to be a preacher. I want to be a sportswriter. I want to be sports announcer on radio or television." Now, I want you to know (I say this way too much) that I'm not making this up. I already was the sports editor of the *North High Oracle.* I was the sports editor. I wrote the articles and took the pictures. I was into journalism, took all the journalism classes the high school had, and sports was a big thing with me.

Later I would be back in church and somewhere in the course of the service, I heard it again:

I want you to be a preacher.

"Lord, Lord—I told you! I'm a Christian. I want to go to heaven—thank God! But I don't want to be a preacher! Lord, I want to be a Christian sportswriter or sports announcer. The big radio station in Des Moines then, and still is, WHO, "the 50,000-watt blowtorch of the Midwest," WHO, 1040 on your dial. I had that thing down! Jim Zabel was the sports anchor of WHO radio and television. I would tell my buddies, "I'm going to take his place someday! I don't want to be a Jim Zabel—I just want to take his place! "

Back to church. Maybe it was a missionary speaking, possibly somebody else, possibly the pastor, and I heard it again:

I want you to be a preacher!

The Lord was trying to get my attention. There was more to this Christian life than asking forgiveness of my sins. He also wanted *my life!* Here's how it came to me: *You have given me your sins—now give me yourself!*

That's a different prayer! That's a prayer of consecration! That's a prayer of "I'll give you me, Lord." I'll tell you the best short scripture along that line, just one verse—Romans 12:1: "I beseech you therefore, brethren, by the mercies of God, that ye present [or give] your bodies a living sacrifice, holy, acceptable unto God, which is your reasonable service" (KJV). You see, that was written to believers. Paul called them "brethren" or "brothers and sisters" in the faith. Their sins had been forgiven! "Now," he said, "I want you to give, present, consecrate, totally give yourself to God! Not just your sins, but yourself!" However, I wanted to be a sports anchor.

I want you to be a preacher!

I fought that all through the school year until the summer. It was camp meeting time, and that means in Iowa all the Nazarenes from the state would come together. There would be a couple thousand of us—great crowds, great music, great preaching. It was quite an event! I got there late Wednesday night because I had a summer job, and the camp meeting was in West Des Moines. As I walked into the back of that great big tabernacle building, the whisper came again, but with different words this time: *Make up your mind: your way or my way!*

I said, "Lord, I'm tired of fighting this thing. Thank you for forgiving me! I'm ready to sell out. If that long-winded preacher will ever get done, I'm willing to head down to the altar and pray."

He finally finished, invited anyone to come forward to pray who wanted to, and I went down that long aisle. I knelt, I cried, I "died out" to being a sports announcer or a sportswriter. I said, "If you want me to be a preacher, let's go. I'll probably die in the last church on the edge of the state and fall off, but let's go!"

I gave myself to God in surrender and consecration. Back when they had that experience in the book of Acts, it was referred to as Pentecost! They were baptized with the Holy Spirit, filled with the

Holy Spirit. A good "Jesus term" is that they were *sanctified by the Holy Spirit.* I don't care what you call it—I want you to say yes to God.

Across the years young people, children, and others have drawn pictures of me preaching. In my office I have a folder of these. These pictures are worth more than a bobblehead of me. I have given my life to the Lord. He has used me to preach the gospel literally around the world, and for the children to respond and draw me in all the ways they have is worth a ton.

Yes, but there's more to it than forgiveness! Give your life to God. His plan is better than your plan! God's plan is the best plan! God bless Jim Zabel. Radio and television may be where God wanted him to serve, but God wanted *me* to be a preacher of the gospel. Remember this phrase: *You have given me your sins—now give me yourself!* Have you done that, my friend?

19 "IF I COULD BE ANYWHERE, I WOULD NOT BE HERE."

Esther 4:14

I was awakened in the night two or three nights ago and started praying about these short messages. "Lord, where do you want me to go; what do you want me to say?" I was reminded of a poem that I had used in the past but I hadn't used for six or eight years. I had to search a little bit but found it. It's written by Jeff Liles, who was a youth pastor when he wrote this. Now he's the senior pastor at the Church of the Nazarene in Kingfisher, Oklahoma. Read this:

If I could be anywhere, I would not be here.
I would be where everyone was nice and kind to
each other.
I would work where nobody threw stones and
nobody cried.
If I could be anywhere, I would not be here.
I would be where no one was lonely and everyone
had at least three friends.
I would be where no one would laugh when I made
a mistake,
And no one comes in last, and everyone gets a
prize for just trying.

If I could be anywhere, I would not be here.
But I am here, so I will bring where I want to be to where I am.
I will find one who makes a mistake and encourage him to keep on trying.
I will look for the lonely and say, "Can I sit with you?"
I will look for tears of hurt and sadness and offer my towel of peace and joy.
I will search for the heartless and give them part of mine.
So if I bring where I want to be to where I am,
Then this is where I need to be!
(Used by permission)

Oh, that is good! Thank you, Jeff! I'm sorry to say that in our beloved United States there are marches in the streets, riots, buildings burning, and graffiti everywhere. Cursing and swearing are heard all the time, so much so that the TV producers have to bleep out about what seems like every other word. Now that's not the America we want. That's not the society we want. It just seems that everybody is on the warpath these days.

Has it dawned on you that God gave you and me life? We're not just animals—we're living souls, and God gave us life. With that life He has us alive in the 2020s. Some of you might wish it were 1920 or why, why didn't I live in 1520? I wonder what it would have been like in 1120. Well, you can go on forever about this, but we're alive in this 21st century. There is a crisis in the land, in the world, and God has you and me here to make a positive difference. If I don't like what's going on, then *I will bring where I want to be to where I am so. . . . Then this is where I need to be!*

I thought, *Where in the world would I find a scripture that would go along with that?* Finally, I'm sure the Lord reminded me of Esther, back in the Old Testament. The story of Esther is about a beautiful young Jewish virgin. The king had gotten rid of the other queen, and then he had all the young ladies gathered together, and from them he chose Esther to be his queen. She was Jewish, but he didn't know that. Then there was an ungodly, evil plot by Haaman to exterminate the Jews by killing every man, woman, and child who were Jewish. Haaman went to the king and presented the plan, and the king went along with his plan to exterminate the Jews.

The word went out, and there was weeping, wailing, and praying across the land. A man named Mordecai went to Esther, the queen, and said (in Esther 4:14), "Yet who knows whether you have come to the kingdom for such a time as this?" (*Who knows, Esther, but what the whole reason that you were chosen was for a time like this to save your people?*)

She agreed to address the king about the situation, knowing that if he didn't like it, he could have her killed on the spot. She said words that we all have heard (Esther 4:16): "If I perish, I perish!" (*I'm going to do what's right.*) She went to the king, who got his eyes opened and saw the true plot that had been orchestrated to eliminate all the Jews. Instead of hanging on the gallows the man whom Haman wanted to hang, the king had Haman himself hung. The Jewish people were spared, and God used Esther to save His people.

How about you? Who knows but that you have come to the kingdom for such a time as this—the 2020s? You are not here by accident and neither am I. Will you stand up and speak up for the Christian worldview—in your office, in the factory, or even on the school board? Wherever you serve in your church, in your neighborhood, or in your city, will you stand up and be an Esther? "If I perish, I perish"—but I'm going to take a stand for righteousness. I'm against what the devil is doing—trying to divide America, divide the world, divide families, and divide marriages. I'm going to take a stand for peace instead of war, for common sense instead of rioting, and for the Jesus worldview instead of the secular worldview. My whole feeling in my heart today is that you're here for a purpose and so am I! We're here not just to stand around and complain about how bad everything is. The Lord has us here to make a difference. I want you to read the last part of Jeff's poem:

> *If I could be anywhere, I would not be here.*
> *But I am here, so I will bring where I want to be*
> *to where I am.*
> *I will find one who makes a mistake and encourage*
> *him to keep on trying.*
> *I will look for the lonely and say, "Can I sit with you?"*
> *I will look for tears of hurt and sadness and offer*
> *my towel of peace and joy.*
> *I will search for the heartless and give them*
> *part of mine.*
> *So if I bring where I want to be to where I am,*
> *Then this is where I need to be!*
> (Used by permission)

My friends, God has you there. God has me here—for a reason. Take courage!

Stand up! Use common sense, but also have courage and boldness.

Read the words of Mordecai to Queen Esther one last time: *Who knows whether you have come to the kingdom for such a time as this?* Don't miss the moment; take courage, speak up, and make a Christ-like difference in your world! God's Holy Spirit will help you!

20 YOU GET TO KEEP ONLY WHAT YOU GIVE AWAY

Mark 8:35

I have one scripture for you today, and one insight or truth. I really pray this will resonate with you. It's the words of Jesus taken from Mark 8:35–36: "Whoever desires to save his life will lose it, but whoever loses his life for My sake and the gospel's will save it. For what will it profit a man if he gains the whole world, and loses his own soul?"

Here's the kingdom premise that I want you to read today: "You get to keep only what you give away!" Think on it just a moment. Again, *you get to keep only what you give away!*

On a plane going to Alexandria, Louisiana, connecting through Dallas, I got on a smaller plane with two seats on each side of the aisle. I came in, it was all open seating, so I sat by the window in the first row. Other people came on and sat wherever they wanted.

The seat by the aisle beside me was empty. The plane took off, and I think we were in the air five, six, or seven minutes when the pilot came on and said, "We're going to be flying into turbulent weather, so flight attendants, please be seated." Everybody buckled up, and a flight attendant, a young lady, came down the aisle and for whatever reason looked at me and said, "I think I'm going to just sit here by you. It's just as good as the jump seat." She got in and fastened her seat belt. I don't know if she saw that I had my New Testament out and was checking some things, but that may have triggered her to ask, "Are you a Christian?"

I said, "I sure am."

She said, "Oh, my. I need to ask some questions. I'm from Minneapolis. I've been going to a Bible study. They're telling me things that I've never heard before. They're telling me that I need to be born again." She looked at me and said, "Do you know anything about that?"

Brother, if that's not an open door to share your faith, you ought to just jump out of the plane.

I said, "Oh, yes! Why, sure!" I gave her a scripture or two that I found there and how Jesus said that we need to repent of our sins and believe on the Lord Jesus Christ and you'll be born again.

I explained it all a whole lot better than I can do right now, and she asked more questions, which I answered. She asked, What about this? What about that? And believe it or not, the plane started descending into Alexandria. She looked at me and said, "Can you believe this? We've been in a storm, and I've been seat-belted since about five or six minutes into the flight. I needed to hear everything you said, so God got us into a storm and got me locked down next to you. You answered every single question, and now the flight is over." She added, "That was no coincidence."

I said, "No, no—that was a God moment." We had a quick kind of "Help us now, Jesus. Bless her, Lord" kind of a prayer and I shook her hand. I've never seen her since, but something happened in my own heart.

I got off the plane, entered the small terminal, the district superintendent met me, and he said, "Hey—good flight?" I said, "Brother, we were in a storm, but did I ever have a chance to tell someone all about how to be born again!" My soul was stirred up; I wanted to go find somebody else to tell.

What's the point? I shared my faith; I gave it away. That's what sharing means, and by doing that, my faith was strengthened! You get to keep only what you give away! So give away your faith by way of a testimony, or *Let me tell you what God did for me.* It strengthens both you and them.

Let me just ask a question or two: Do you want to live with forgiveness and acceptance from others? Well, then—you have to forgive and accept other people. If you don't forgive, if you have resentment, and if you're carrying a grudge, it's no wonder nobody forgives you. You keep only what you give away. How about your self-esteem? Would you like your self-esteem to be raised? Let me give you a kindergarten point right here about what you can do. Quit feeling sorry for yourself. Quit saying, "Poor me," and "Nothing good ever happens to me." Quit talking like that and start reaching out. Compliment somebody else, encourage somebody else, help somebody else, and your own self-esteem starts to rise.

Do you want your financial needs met? Well, let me tell you the words of Jesus that He said from the book of Luke: "Give, and it will be given to you, pressed down, shaken together, and running over will be put into your bosom. For with the same measure that you use, it will be measured back to you" (Luke 6:38).

This is *not* "give to get"—no, no! This is giving to Christ and the kingdom, and God is saying, "You can't outgive me. Give and I'll give it back to you!"

I was with a group of people and felt strongly led to get into my billfold, take a $50 bill out, and give it to a couple I knew who I realized needed some help. This was not church money; this was my money. I gave it to them; they couldn't believe it. We all hugged each other. I think they cried a little bit. I left, got back into the car, and felt good in my heart. I helped somebody and it helped me. It'll give you joy. A week or so later somebody sent me a note from another state that said, "I don't know why I'm doing this, but I feel so led to send you a check. It is enclosed. God bless you!" The check was for $50! I said, "I just gave it away last week." I went down to the bank and cashed the check for a $50 bill. I folded it, put it in my billfold, and said, "I'm going to give that thing out again." If you know me very well at all, you know I've given away $50 bills over and over for years. I've given $50 to many of the missionaries I've met throughout the world over the years. They all looked amazed—"What are you doing?" God has ways of giving that money back to me, and it would take three more of these "Refuels" to explain all that.

My whole point is this: *Keep it and you're going to lose it. Give it away and you'll have it—because God is in this program.* Amen! Share this with somebody else. Go do something for somebody today, and you know what you get for it? A joyful heart! You get to keep only what you give away! Give away some love and you'll end up being loved! It's the gospel truth!

21 THE UNKNOWN BUNDLE

1 Kings 17:2–3

The Lord has brought a phrase back to my mind that I have not thought of in months and probably years. I heard this a lot as a young fellow growing up in my home church back in Iowa either from the pastor or from the evangelist who would come. Here it is: *Put it in the unknown bundle.*

I know that doesn't make much sense to start with, but consider the *whys*—"Why this?" "Why did that happen?" "Why, Lord?" "Why did you let that happen?" Do you know that God doesn't give us the answer to the *whys* or the *how comes*? Old-time preachers used to say, "Just put it in the unknown bundle, place that bundle on God's altar, and let it be surrendered to God—because you'll never figure out all the *whys*."

It occurs to me that even Jesus on the cross asked, "My God, my God, why have you forsaken me?" I don't find anywhere in Scripture where God ever answered that question. Jesus simply had to surrender it to the Father.

Let me give you an illustration or two. I was a young pastor in our second pastorate. Things were going well, and there was a professor who was an evangelist coming from Bethany Nazarene College (now Southern Nazarene University) by the name of Paul McGrady. Our district superintendent had him at our camp meeting as the evangelist. There was always great singing, and Paul McGrady would preach and kick his foot. He had more joy and more enthusiasm than I had ever seen from any other preacher. Camp meeting would be over, but he was going to be back next year and I knew I would get to hear Paul McGrady again. He left an indelible mark on me.

I went up to him after one of the services and asked him if he would come to our rather small church for a revival meeting. He put his arm around me and said, "Sure, I'll come!" We settled on a date and I was one excited young pastor! We were going to get Paul McGrady at our church! In the summer before the time for him to come to us, he was in the college van with a men's quartet from the college. They were on their way to another engagement where the quartet would sing and he would preach. A terrible car wreck occurred in Tulsa, and Paul McGrady was killed along with the quartet members.

Paul McGrady was doing such a great work (he was only in his 40s), and it shook me to my foundation. Why would God let Paul McGrady get caught in a terrible car wreck when he was the most effective preacher I had ever known? Another pastor said to me, "You have to put it in the unknown bundle and give it to God—because you're never going to figure out why." That was a tough one for me!

Now I'll jump ahead a few more years. My friend Tom Bailey and I had been soulmate buddies for thirty years. He was my confidant, my pal, really my soulmate friend. He called me on a Thursday and said, "They've discovered some kind of a brain tumor and I've got to go in for exploratory surgery just in order to find out what kind of a tumor it is and so they'll know how to treat it." Then he added, "Hey, old buddy—I'll call you Saturday because I'm only in the hospital for a day. Be praying for me." Well, I did pray—but can you believe that Tom Bailey died on the operating table? My pal was only fifty-eight years old.

"Lord, Lord—why take him?"

Now let me tell you about the prophet Elijah. First Kings 17 tells us that Elijah confronted wicked king Ahab. God told the prophet, "You tell that wicked king that there will be no rain until I give the word because of his wickedness and leading my people to the devil." The prophet did exactly what God told him to do and gave the king that word of judgment from the Lord. Of course, they then wanted to kill the prophet!

"Then the word of the Lord came to him, saying, 'Get away from here and turn eastward, and hide by the Brook Cherith, which flows into the Jordan. And it will be that you shall drink from the brook, and I have commanded the ravens to feed you there.' So he went and did according to the word of the Lord, for he went and stayed by the Brook Cherith, which flows into the Jordan. The ravens brought him bread and meat in the morning, and bread and meat in the evening; and he drank from the brook" (1 Kings 17:2–6). Then, the next verse (7) says, "And it happened after a while that the brook dried up, because there had been no rain in the land."

Can't you hear Elijah saying, "Lord, you told me to come here. You told me to hide by the brook and stay away from the wicked king and I obeyed. I did what you said and now the brook is dried up. Lord, this doesn't make any sense." He said to the Lord, "Why did you send me out here? The brook dried up. You surely realized that in your foreknowledge." The question is "What do you do when the brook dries up?" There's more to the story and I'll finish it next time.

My burden for you today is *What do you do when the brook dries up?* If you don't put it in the unknown bundle and place it on the altar of God, then you start getting cynical, critical, and skeptical.

I have more "why" stories to share, but the point is *Have you surrendered it to God? Have you put that mystery in the unknown bundle? Is your unknown bundle on God's altar?* God has never promised to answer all our *whys,* but He has promised to walk with us through those dark valleys. By the way, God didn't let Elijah stay by that dried up brook and die. I'll tell you about that another time. And neither will God abandon *you*!

22 GOD BROUGHT GOOD OUT OF BAD—AGAIN

1 Kings 17:9–16

Last time I was talking about Elijah the prophet of God in 1 Kings and how he had to confront Ahab the wicked king. The king was going to kill Elijah, so God directed Elijah to go hide by the brook Cherith. God told him He would feed him and that the ravens would bring him the food and he would drink from the brook. The problem was that a drought was on and the brook dried up. I put the tag on last week's message as "the unknown bundle." Why did God lead him there and then all of a sudden it became a disaster? Why do a lot of things happen to us? That's where we were last time; so now we'll just hook on right there and go forward.

Elijah the prophet was a man of prayer, and in the New Testament book of James we read, "Elijah was a man like us." He was not an angel or a divine being but rather a human being just like us. He prayed earnestly that it would not rain, and it did not rain in the land for three years and six months. Then he prayed again and the heavens gave rain (James 5:17–18).

What did he do in the wilderness when the brook Cherith dried up? There's not a doubt in my mind that he prayed, "What do I do now, Lord?" Here is what I strongly feel is the direction that the

Holy Spirit wants to whisper to a lot of people right now: *Pray and wait.* Wait for what? Wait for the still, small voice of the Holy Spirit to tell you what to do next. By the way, this truth is brought out in First Kings 17 where the Holy Spirit whispered to Elijah about what to do next.

The Bible doesn't tell us how long Elijah had to wait by the brook. Sometimes the time we have to wait is short and sometimes it's long. Then the Lord spoke to him: "Arise, go to Zarephath . . . and dwell there. I have commanded a widow there to provide for you" (v. 9). Elijah got up and headed toward Zarephath. Friends, I had to look it up, and the scholars say it was about a hundred miles away. They didn't have any interstates. They didn't have any cars. I don't know if he walked or if he had donkey or a horse. Either way, one hundred miles there in the desert would be tough, even when God nudges us as to what to do. It doesn't mean it's going to be easy.

Elijah finally got to Zarephath, and sure enough, the widow was out collecting sticks to make a fire. The scripture tells us that he asked her to bring him a cup of water. The man was probably about to pass out because of thirst! As she started to go in and get it, Elijah added, "Also bring me a morsel of bread in your hand" (v. 11).

The little widow lady said, "As the Lord your God lives, I do not have bread, only a handful of flour in a bin, and a little oil in a jar; and see, I am gathering a couple of sticks that I may go in and prepare it for myself and my son, that we may eat it, and die" (v. 12). Listen to what the prophet said to her: "Do not fear; go and do as you have said, but make me a small cake from it first, and bring it to me; and afterward make some for yourself and your son. For thus says the Lord God of Israel: 'The bin of flour shall not be used up, nor shall the jar of oil run dry, until the day the Lord sends rain on the earth'" (vv. 13–14).

The Bible says she obeyed and got the flour and oil, made a little cake, and brought it to Elijah. The miracle of that story is that the flour didn't run out and the oil didn't run out for three and a half years, when the rain started again, just as the prophet had promised!

Let's review: God directed Elijah to the brook Cherith; then the brook dried up. Next the Lord said, "Now I have another plan—I'll get you to Zarephath." In Zarephath was a widow lady, desperately poor, and she had a little son. She also had an upstairs bedroom, which she gave to Elijah. That's better than sleeping by a brook! Elijah also had somebody to talk to, and that's better than being out there in the wilderness all alone. Then he had home-cooked meals—those were undoubtedly better than what the birds had brought him to eat. On top of all of that, Elijah had a little boy to torment and to tease. Now he's got a bedroom, a little boy to have fun with, home-made meals, and somebody to talk to. I can hear Elijah say, "The best thing that ever happened to me was when the brook dried up!" God turned bad into good again!

When I arrived at one of my pastorates, I soon found out the church was in critical shape financially. In fact, an auditor told me, "You are one step away from bankruptcy." It's far too much to explain in detail, but for the first number of months I did everything possible to reduce the church's expenditures and increase the church's income. We finally, finally crawled out of "the red" and were current on all our bills.

We were starting to see light at the end of the tunnel and then—a sheriff's deputy arrived at the church. He asked me if I was the pastor of the church. When I answered yes, he said, "Then this lawsuit goes to you." The church had been sued for many thousands of dollars by a former staff member for wage and sex discrimination. I looked at that judgment against us, went back into my office, closed the door, and wept. I knew that would sink us!

"Why, why, Lord? After all the church and I have done to get out of the red financially, *why this now?* Lord, I don't even know the lady. Why didn't she bring the suit when the former pastor was here? *He* hired her—I didn't. Why, Lord?"

To make a very long story very short, we finally went to arbitration. It was agreed by both parties that the amount of the suit would be reduced to half, but it would be due in thirty days. I had to go before our congregation the next Sunday to explain our crisis, stating that we must raise multi-thousands of dollars in thirty days, but I couldn't give the amount needed because of a gag order by the judge.

The crowd responded! We all started putting checks into the offering plates marked "Litigation Offering." I would tell the congregation each Sunday during the next month that we were 20-percent there, 50-percent there, 70-percent there—and then the last Sunday of the month came. A young mother in the church handed me her check out in the hallway. She gave a very generous amount and in the memo line of the check she wrote, "Litigation Offering—BOOOO!" I laughed out loud and asked her to explain it. She said, "I absolutely don't believe in suing the church! But I love my church, and therefore I'm giving." On that last Sunday of the month we went over the top and the judgment was paid. Praise God forever!

As I look back on that crisis I see (1) it brought the congregation together; (2) people went to urgent prayer; (3) young and old, wealthy, and poor—everyone gave sacrificially; and (4) we all learned once again that "God is bigger than even an unjust lawsuit." God brought good out of bad . . . again!

Now, you finish this sentence with your own "impossibility"—"God is bigger than ____________!" Never forget it: *God is bigger!* I'm still rejoicing over that miracle from God, given through sacrificial, obedient Christians!

23 LESSONS LEARNED THROUGH THE DEATH OF DAVE

John 14:27

God teaches a lot of different ways, and one of the ways was very painful for me as it came about in lessons I learned from the death of our son Dave. You may not be in grief, but you likely know somebody who is. It may be grief from the loss of a son or daughter, it may be due to a terrible divorce that has recently hit you or a friend of yours, or it may be from the loss of a beloved dad or mom or someone else close to you. I just felt led to give you some of the lessons I learned. You may need this, or someone you know may need it.

A few years ago our son Dave found out that he had melanoma cancer. For two years we went through the fight. We did everything known to man. It came down to a Monday morning in a hospital in Colorado Springs. I was there, having just flown in from Canada to get there before his likely death. The family was all there, including Lori, his wife, and their girls. At 9:20 that morning Dave died. Our boy died. There wasn't any 11:59 midnight miracle, as I had prayed; Dave died. A month after his death I started thinking, "Lord, were you trying to teach me something through that ordeal?" Before that,

I don't think I was listening in that regard. The following are some of lessons I learned.

Lesson number one: *We can't make it through the dark valleys of life without God and God's people.* We've all gone through hard things, and God has helped us. He's the one who brings comfort, grace, strength, healing, and ultimately peace. But I learned that we also need *God's people* to help us. The calls that came, the letters, the cards, the emails, the other communication, the tears, the hugs—they were all so helpful. As the little boy said, " I need Jesus with skin on to come and help me." I learned we need God and we need God's people, and you are some of those people—so reach out to others in grief.

The second lesson learned was this: *Believers don't really die.* When Dave stopped breathing in that hospital room in Colorado Springs, I went to the window, weeping, and said to the Lord, "It's over. I guess we're not going to have a last-minute miracle." A whisper from the Holy Spirit came into my mind: *Dave didn't die!* What? *Dave didn't die.* No, he just changed his address from Colorado Springs to heaven!

I went back to the bed with the family all gathered around and said, "Dave didn't die!" They looked at me like *What?* I said, "I just got the word from the Lord—Dave just changed his address from Colorado Springs to heaven! The body died, but the real Dave Diehl has gone on to be with Jesus. Thanks be to God!" As Paul said, to be absent from the body is to be present with the Lord (see 2 Corinthians 5:8). That lesson helped me immensely.

Lesson number three: *God actually did heal Dave but not the way I thought He should.* I was looking for healing now, and the Lord said, "Let me heal him forever," and then I started to see that. Dave will never again have cancer. He will never again have pain or suffering. About a month later it hit me—Dave will never be disappointed ever again! Praise God! That is a permanent healing! Take courage in that—it's a forever healing!

Number four: *Everyone grieves differently.* The cards, letters and calls started coming to us from everywhere because I've been around the world quite a few times and have many friends. Dorothy, my wife, couldn't read the cards for weeks because all she would do would be to cry and sob. We simply had to stack the cards up, and about a month later she started reading them. That's an illustration of grieving differently. The cards did me good day after day and I looked forward to going to the mailbox—but Dorothy couldn't read them for a month or more. Just mark it down in lessons learned: "Don't make everyone grieve the way you think they should!"

Lesson number five: *Great love brings great grief.* If you've had great love for the person who has died (or even walked out on you), then there's going to be great grief. If there is little love, there's little grief. I just said this last week to a lady in Tennessee: "God bless you, because I know you loved greatly—so you grieve greatly." I thank God! Let's go ahead and love greatly, because God is going to help us come through the grief!

Lesson number six: *People grieving deeply won't read big books.* I didn't know that until I went through grief. Some people gave me some big books, but I had no interest in them. A little booklet was given to me, *Good Grief,* by Granger Westberg, which was written fifty or sixty years ago. I've read it over and over many times. I've given out dozens of copies of that booklet, having learned that a grieving mind can't handle long speeches or big books. It needs to be a short speech or book, a hug, or sharing tears.

That brings me to my lesson seven: *Don't say, "I understand what you're going through and here's what you ought to do"*—unless you've gone through a similar loss. If you've never lost a child, don't go to someone who just did and act as if you know everything he or she ought to do, because you don't. One of the most valued letters I received came from David and Charlene Adams from Indiana: "Dear Dr. Diehl and Dorothy:" (If you could see it, you would notice that it's an empty page.) At the bottom of the page they had written, "We love you deeply," and signed it. I looked at that and looked at that and said to myself, *They forgot to write anything.* Then it dawned on me that through that blank page they were saying, *We've never gone through what you've gone through. We've never lost a child. All we can say is that we love you.* Wow! That empty letter spoke volumes to me.

After Dave died we got through the funeral and through the initial grief of it. I was back out, going around the country preaching as I do, and the devil started harassing me: "Why did God heal you but not heal your boy?" You see, about ten years earlier I had been healed of thyroid cancer. It was a problem for sure; I'll tell you about that miracle later in this book. The devil was echoing in my mind when I would be out across the country and in a lonely hotel or motel room: "Why did God heal you but not heal your boy?" He was trying to steal my peace, just as he's trying to do to you—trying to steal your joy too.

I was at once in a small-town church and saw that the sanctuary was empty. I started walking back and forth in front of the altar, saying, "Lord, why didn't you let *me* die? Dave had a wife and two little girls." I felt the Lord whispering to me, "Give Dave to me." I went out to the car, got my Bible, brought it in, opened it to where Dave's picture was, and there was Dave and Lori with the girls. I put the picture of my boy on the altar and said, "I give him to you, God! I give Dave to you!" You may not believe this, but I picked up the picture, put it back into my Bible, walked out of the sanctuary—and I had peace in my heart. It's still there now. God gave me peace!

The last lesson, lesson eight, that I learned is this: *God's greatest gift to His children is His peace.* Read John 14:27 carefully now, the words of Jesus: "Peace I leave with you, My peace I give to you; not as the world gives do I give to you. Let not your heart be troubled, neither let it be afraid." Jesus still brings peace! Praise the Lord!

Some of you are feeling discouraged; Satan is trying to steal your peace. Maybe you need to give something to God. Do it now—give it to God! Read what Jesus said three times in John 20: *Peace be with you, peace be with you, peace be with you!* Anytime Jesus says something three times, you know He is emphasizing it.

Jesus Christ our Lord will give you peace. We have to work through the grief process and release it to God piece by piece. Don't give up!

Yes, there will always be a hole in your heart after your loved one or soulmate friend leaves, but the Comforter will wrap His arms around you and bring you peace—*if* you let Him. We serve a healing God!

24 LESSONS LEARNED FROM OTHERS IN THE VALLEY OF GRIEF

Psalm 30:5

Last time I shared with you some of the lessons that I learned through the death of Dave, and I've heard from many of you about that and I appreciate your responses. I learned a long time ago that there is wisdom in the crowd, and I want to pick up on what some of you have said because there's wisdom in what you have shared with me.

Rev. Joe McNulty, pastor of Cornerstone Church of the Nazarene in Cullman, Alabama, wrote, "Grief is very personal and is no respecter of persons. Everyone grieves differently; don't try to rush yourself through the process. Just because a certain amount of time has gone by doesn't mean that you should be over it." I ought to add that Rev. McNulty was on staff at Children's Hospital in Birmingham, Alabama, for many years and was quite involved in grief counseling there.

He went on to quote Rabbi Harold Kushner: "At some of the darkest moments of my life, some people that I thought were my friends deserted me, some because they cared about me and it hurt them to see me in pain, others because I reminded them of their own vulnerability, and it was more than they could handle. Real friends overcame their discomfort and came to sit with me. If they had no words to make me feel better, they sat in silence and I loved them for it. . . . *Sometimes it's not what we say that matters—it's our presence."* That is a tremendous lesson learned, and you can do that for others who are going through hard times. If you can't be there physically, you can be there by a note or by phone—the gift of presence, *your* presence!

Esther Crabtree of Springfield, Ohio, wrote, "Singing has always brought me joy, but when Jim, my husband, died, my song was gone. I couldn't sing for two years." Her husband was an outstanding evangelist whom many will remember, Rev. Jim Crabtree. I didn't know that when Jim died, Esther couldn't sing for two years. That's a powerful truth right there—we all grieve differently, and sometimes grief takes the song out of our heart, but may it not be forever. By the way, Esther is now singing and playing the piano every Sunday at her church. God brought her song back.

Rev. Danny Goddard, pastor of First Church of the Nazarene in New Castle, Indiana, conducts a seminar called "Living with Your Loss." He said, "Death is not the only cause of grief. It could be a breakup, a divorce, the selling of a childhood home, the loss of a dream, infertility, a job loss, the end of a career, or the loss of a beloved pet. Regardless of the type of grief, the loss must be acknowledged and only then can healing begin." I never would have understood that the loss of a pet would bring grief, but at my stage in life in which little Kasey is the life of our house, now I understand.

Cindy Lamb of Colorado Springs Colorado, wrote about the death of her infant son Evan. "My family felt it was best to avoid talking about Evan. I disagree. We need to share our feelings, memories, and pains with others. Don't avoid talking about the deceased! It's healing to talk about him or her." I agree, and we have pictures of our son nearby. We don't try to hide that he is still part of our lives.

Mark Murphy, my friend from Selma, Indiana, sent this tremendous truth: “Grief never ends, but it changes; it’s a passage, not a place to stay. Grief is not a sign of weakness or a lack of faith—it’s the price of love!”

I have been thinking for several days of Psalm 30:5—"Weeping may endure for a night, but joy comes in the morning.” I’ve also been singing that Gaither song these days: “Hold on, my child; joy comes in the morning!”

As Mark Murphy said, grief changes; it’s a passage, not a place to stay. Esther Crabtree was in the valley of grief for two years, but thank God, joy comes in the morning! However, the psalmist didn’t tell us how long the night would be. It could be two or three weeks, it could be two or three months, it could be two or three years, but the night *will* end and joy will come in the morning—if you give your loss to Christ and commit all to Him and let His peace flood your soul!

If you’re going through the valley of grief, don’t hide from God, and don’t hide from people. God will ultimately bring you peace, and often He speaks to us through loving people.

A loving God and loving people—we need both! Don’t find a cave and hide. There is no peace there. *Joy comes in the morning!*

25 SHOW ME, TEACH ME, LEAD ME

Psalm 25:4–5

Today we are going to Psalm 25, and without reading it all, let me tell you about David when he was the king of Judah. He was being chased again by an enemy and was crying out to God for help. In verses 1–3 he writes, "To You, O Lord, I lift up my soul. O my God, I trust in You; Let me not be ashamed; Let not my enemies triumph over me. I deed, let no one who waits on You be ashamed; Let those be ashamed who deal treacherously without cause." In verse 16 he goes on: "Turn Yourself to me, and have mercy on me, for I am desolate and afflicted."

Can't you hear the cry of the king to the Lord? He was probably in a cave somewhere as he wrote this. David continues: "The troubles of my heart have enlarged; bring me out of my distresses!" (v. 17). Have you ever felt like that?—"Help me, Lord! Help! What else can I say, what else can I do?" That's the way Psalm 25 reads except for two verses, verses 4 and 5.

It's as if he just put parentheses in the plea and said, "Show me Your ways, O Lord; Teach me Your paths. Lead me in Your truth." Then he went right back to pleading: "Do not remember the sins of my youth" (v. 7). That little parenthesis prayer fits us today. I pray this prayer more than you'll ever know: "Show me, Lord, what you want me to do; Teach me, Lord. Lead me, Lord!"

Those three thoughts came out of the heart of a king who was crying for mercy. What an insight: "Show me your way, Lord!" It seems to me that there are so many forks in the road. *Do I go this way? Do I go that way? Do you want me to say yes to that? No to that? Show me, Lord. Show me!*

Personally, Dorothy and I were in several forks in the road ourselves. Should we keep this home, which is fairly sizable, or was it time to downsize and to get into something much smaller? Fork in the road: What shall we do? When I did this originally, we were at a fork in the road about these videos. Was I supposed to go on and do this, or had we come to a point where we were being this far through the pandemic that it was time to move on to something else? Obviously the end was coming, but God had a plan to get this book out to keep the messages going. That prayer fits all of us. Pray about whatever situation, whatever fork in the road, "Show me, Lord," and He will!

The next prayer is "Teach me in your paths." I read what the scholars have to say, and they said this is not an account or a picture of a teacher or professor saying, "Listen up, fellows and girls. You really need to hear this, so listen. I'm going to teach you something." No, they said this is a picture of asking the Lord to teach us while we walk together on the path with Him. *Lord, as we walk together on this journey, what do you want to teach me today? What are you trying to teach me in these hard times?* I was going through agony concerning the death of our son Dave. I'll be honest—I was not praying, "Teach me something, Lord." I was under too much grief for that. However, after the death and after a while of walking the path of grief,

I started praying, "What do you want to teach me, Lord? What do I need to learn?"

I was at Crossroads Church of the Nazarene in North Chesterfield, Virginia, and the people heard me talk about Dave's death. They said, "Write that up—we want that because we have a grief recovery ministry." So I wrote "15 Truths Learned from the Dying of Dave." The Lord taught me what I had never known before about the valley of grief. *Lord, show me which way to go! Lord, teach me as we walk the path! Lead me.*

The New International Version translation tells us, "Guide me in your truth and teach me" (v. 5). The Lord leads us through the promptings of His Holy Spirit and His nudges. He also leads us through His checks: "Don't do that again. Don't go there again. Don't say that again!" Thank God for the "checks of the Spirit."

It was a Friday in our home. I felt nudged, I felt prompted, that we needed to go to Dave's grave. Friday afternoon on Wadsworth Boulevard is not the time to make a quick trip across town! It's traffic rush time and we're at the south end of Lakewood and the cemetery is just beyond the north end of Lakewood.

I said to Dorothy, "I don't know why, but we need to go see if Dave's grave is okay and if Dave is okay." We got in the car, took our little dog with us, and headed to the cemetery through rush-hour traffic. I got out of the car and started walking around the gravesite, brushing a few leaves off the tombstone. A pickup truck pulled up and a man got out and started walking straight toward us. I had never seen the man before, so I just said, "Hello. You must have somebody out here in the cemetery you're coming to visit."

He looked at me and said, "My sweetheart. We were only a month from our big wedding anniversary, and my sweetheart died." Imagine my surprise. The burial site was directly behind Dave's. I honestly hadn't even picked up on that; the dirt was still fresh. He was coming out to put some flowers on the grave of his sweetheart.

I responded, "This is where our son Dave is buried."

He said to me, "You know, I'm a retired pastor, and it's easier to tell people how to handle grief than to handle it yourself."

I said, "Friend, I'm also a retired pastor. I understand what you're saying—it's easier to tell others than to go through it yourself. Dorothy, come over here and bring the dog." We got together, and there was Dorothy, the retired pastor, and me with arms around each other, and we started praying for each another.

There were tears, there were hugs, and he said, "I can't believe this. I can't believe that you've gone through this. You know my lifestyle and I know about your life." We had never met. We hugged each other, slapped each other on the backs, and I said, "God bless you, man!" The Lord's going to get you through your grief as He's going to get us through ours."

We got in the car and headed for home, and I said to Dorothy, "God had us there at that exact moment to minister to that brother." That's what I mean about being led by the Spirit. Obey those prompts, those nudges! "Show me your way; teach me as we walk the path; lead me, O God!"

Why not start praying that prayer every day? *Show me. Teach me. Lead me.* King David gave us that simple prayer that I've learned to pray every day. Will you join me?

26 THINGS MISSING IN HEAVEN

Revelation 21:1–7

I've lost many, too many, of my friends recently from death. Several of them were pastors, pastor's spouses, and laypeople. I've been to too many funerals lately, so my mind started working on heaven. I realize I'm not forty-five years old anymore, but I think more people my general age are in heaven than are still here. So I started thinking about heaven and opened up the Scriptures to Revelation, and that's where I want to show you some truths today that have come to me.

First, let me just give you this little bit of background. John wrote the gospel of John and 1, 2, and 3 John, and then that beloved disciple of Jesus was exiled to Patmos. Patmos is an island in the Mediterranean made mostly of rocks, and that's where the Roman powers would send criminals, political enemies, or anybody they didn't like. They would exile them to Patmos to shrivel up, suffer, and die. That's what they did with John—sent him to Patmos and thought that nobody would ever hear from him again. However, John got to the Isle of Patmos and God gave him the greatest vision of the end times as to what's after this earthly life. I believe it was the greatest vision ever viewed by man. It is what we call the book of Revelation.

It's surprising, but when he saw the new Jerusalem and heaven, John started listing things that were *not* there. Therefore, the title here today is "Things Missing in Heaven." Let's pick it up with verse 4: "And God will wipe away every tear from their eyes." *No more tears,* thank God—*no more crying!* There will be *no more death!* Could I just stop and say—when we make it to heaven there will be *no more funerals!* Thank the Lord! *No more caskets, no more burials, no more death, nor sorrow or crying.* There shall be *no more pain!* Some of you ought to say, "Amen," out loud to that. Some of you are in pain right now. I'm going to say, "Thank God—I'll have no more kidney stone pain, no more gout pain, no more bladder spasm pain." You name it, no more pain in heaven—"for the former things have passed away."

In verse 1 John wrote, "I saw a new heaven and a new earth, for the first heaven and the first earth had passed away. Also there was no more sea." *No sea.* I know I've read that a hundred times and didn't understand what was meant by "no sea." That was until I read a book by Henry Jowett, English author and preacher, who said the reason John said there was no more sea was that the sea surrounded Patmos and to John that represented separation—separation from all his family, from the band of early Christians, from everyone he loved and knew. The sea meant separation. "I'm alone; I can't be with anybody I know or love"—and here in this chapter John said first thing, "There was no more sea." Just write in your Bible sometime, *no more separation from our loved ones in heaven!*

Here are some things I've added to the list of things that won't be in heaven. First, *no more disappointments.* When our son Dave died at age 45, it was a week or two after his death and funeral that it came to me, "Dave will never be disappointed again!" He worked with people, and people will disappoint you. Now some more things that won't be in heaven. Thank God, *no more hunger.* Think about that. Also, *no more poverty.* No, there's going to be plenty in heaven! *No more wars.* Thank you, Jesus! I was born just before World War II, then there's the Korean War, the Vietnam War, the Six-Day War over Israel and thereabouts, the Gulf wars, the Middle East desert wars, and then the invisible war against COVID-19! *No more riots, no more drugs, no more forest fires burning California and the rest of the western US.* There will be *no more floods, no more hurricanes, no more tornadoes, no more loneliness, and no more sin or sorrow or Satan!*

Let me just tell you: "There shall by no means enter it anything that defiles, or causes an abomination or a lie, but only those who are written in the Lamb's Book of Life" (v. 27). I need to say to you today—and read this carefully—I want *you* to be in heaven. Jesus wants you to be in heaven! He died on the cross to pay your penalty for sins so that you can be in heaven. Don't be lost in the devil's hell! Jesus wants *you*; I want you in heaven. However, you have to do more than sign a card, join a church, or simply be a nice guy or gal. Again, your name has to be "written in the Lamb's Book of Life"! How do you get your name in that book? You ask forgiveness of your sins from Jesus Christ, our Lord. Believe on the Lord Jesus Christ as your Savior and Lord. Give your life to Him, and He comes into your very innermost being, and your name is written in that book! Praise God! By the way, there's no Baptist part of heaven, Catholic part of heaven, or Nazarene part of heaven. No, no, no, no! It's for those whose sins have been washed away by the blood of Jesus Christ. We're all going to die, but heaven will be worth it all!

Praise God and be encouraged. Some of you have lost loved ones recently. I grieve with you, but don't grieve long for your loved ones—if they knew Jesus, they're in God's great heaven, and it lasts forever! The whole point is, this world is not all there is! This world is not my home—I'm heading to an eternal home. Come go with me!

Share this with somebody who really needs to be reminded that heaven is still real. We have loved ones there. I'll see you before heaven, I hope, but let's live for Jesus! Heaven is ahead for God's people. Praise God! Amen!

27 OUR LAMPS ARE GOING OUT!

Matthew 25

In Matthew 25 Jesus told a story about a wedding back in His time in that culture. He explained that the bridegroom would be coming to receive the bride at her house and would have his friends, or his attendants, go with him from his home to the bride's home. They would then take the bride and her ten or more attendants, each attendant, or virgin, having a lamp (or torch). They would have fire burning in the lamps as they left the house with the bridegroom and his gentlemen leading the group back to the bridegroom's home for the marriage supper. The virgins would skip, jump, or dance along with their lamps burning. It was a festive time!

In Jesus's story five of the virgins were described as wise and five as foolish. The wise had taken oil with them for their lamps. However, the bridegroom tarried, not coming when they thought he would. It was evidently evening in this story because otherwise the lamps would not have been illuminated much in the daytime. As they were waiting they got tired and finally all fell asleep.

At midnight the cry was heard: "Behold—the bridegroom is here!" The ten virgins all jumped up and trimmed their lamps, making sure their fire was burning as it should. But the foolish virgins, who had brought no oil with them, said to the wise ones, "Give us some of your oil, for our lamps are going out."

The wise ones replied, "No, we can't do that. If we did, there wouldn't be enough for us and you both. Go to the sellers and buy some for yourselves."

"While they went to buy, the bridegroom came, and those who were ready"—let me repeat: *those who were ready*—"went in with him to the wedding; and the door was shut" (Matthew 25:10). Afterwards the other virgins (the five foolish ones) came saying, "Open to us! Open to us!" But the bridegroom said, "I don't know you!" Jesus concluded the story by warning, "Watch therefore, for you know neither the day nor the hour in which the Son of Man is coming" (v. 13).

There are huge truths in this story told by Jesus. First of all, ten virgins had ten lamps. The lamp is a symbol of our profession spiritually." Yes, of course I'm a Christian. What do you think I am? A Buddhist, an atheist, a Muslim? No, I'm a Christian—here's my lamp."

There was fire in the lamps, but the fire was going out and the foolish virgins hadn't brought any oil with them. In the Scriptures oil is a symbol of the Holy Spirit. Dear friends, brother, sister, young person, here's the truth that screams out to us today: You have to have *more* than a lamp! You have to have *more* than a profession! There must be *fire in your soul,* and that fire is maintained by the oil of the Holy Spirit. The question today is not "Do you have a lamp?" The question is "Is there any fire in your lamp?" "Is there any flame in your soul?"

Or has the flame gone out? Has it all gone cold? Friends, that's what Jesus was saying. They had their lamps—but the fire was going out and there was no oil to keep the fire burning.

Here is another lesson: You can't get to heaven on borrowed religion. "Lord God, don't you know who my dad is? Don't you know who my mom is? I mean, she's as godly as you can get." That's wonderful, but that won't get you or me into heaven. Is there a fire in *your* soul?

Let me switch the analogy from a lamp to a lighthouse. The lamp in this illustration was to give light in the darkness. A lighthouse is to give light in the darkness and to guide people to a safe haven. Let's say we have one lighthouse that has the light on, the fire is burning, and the beam is shining out. Another lighthouse has no light in it. It's dark and dead inside. If Jesus would have used this as an analogy, he would say, "You are the lighthouse. Is there any light shining?"

Does the oil of the Holy Spirit reign in your heart and life? Is the light coming through? Does the light shine through your countenance? Does it shine through your attitude and your words? I really want you to understand this simple analogy—do you have the lights on? Is the Holy Spirit giving the light that must shine from within you? Or is your lighthouse dark? I want to tell you that He hasn't returned yet. There's time to pray. There's time to say, "Lord, bring back the light!"

Don't point to your lighthouse and simply say, "Don't I look good?" *Is there a fire burning?*

The point I'm making is a question: "Is there a fire burning in your lighthouse? Is your soul alive and burning because the oil of the Holy Spirit is in total control? Don't live carrying around a dark lamp (lighthouse). *Keep the fire burning!*

28 "IF ONLY"; "WHAT IF?"

Numbers 14:2

No matter who you are or who I am, Satan is out to steal our peace. Oh, brother—can I get an amen for that? The devil is out to steal our peace, our joy, and in the long run he wants to steal our souls. I want you to think with me for a few minutes now on two tactics, two weapons the devil uses against almost all of us. He's out to steal our peace and beyond. Okay, it's not too complicated, so here we go.

The first weapon the devil uses (and he's been doing this for centuries) comes with two simple words: *If only.* Yes, *If only. If only* I'd never moved to this town. *If only* I had graduated when I had a chance. Now, we need to be careful with this one—*If only* I had never married her or married him. *If only* I wouldn't have done that stupid thing—that was more than stupid; it was wrong. *If only I had . . . If only I had not . . .* If only!

The devil is using this to steal your peace about something in the past. I want you to know that this is in the Bible—Numbers 14. The children of Israel, the Jewish nation, had been in bondage and captivity in Egypt for 400 years. Moses had led them out of Egypt and now was leading them to freedom, to the promised land. Then there was the miracle of the Red Sea. Then on and on, and now they are at the border of the promised land, what we would know as Israel today. Moses sent twelve spies to go into the land for forty days to check it out. They came back; ten of them had a terrible report while two of them had a positive report. The ten said, "We can't do it; we can't go in there. They have walled cities. The people are giants. We'll be like grasshoppers in their sight. We can't go."

That whole crowd, that whole generation of the children of Israel started weeping, murmuring, and yelling at Moses. Look at the Bible now: "All the children of Israel complained against Moses and Aaron, and the whole congregation said to them, 'If only we had died in the land of Egypt! Or if only we had died in this wilderness!'" (Numbers 14:2). *If only we had died, we wouldn't be in this mess today, and now we've got giants who are going to eat us up and walled cities that we can't overcome.*

My friend, they had apparently forgotten all the miracles that God had done for them in their generation. *If only, if only.* I want to tell you today—quit saying that to yourself! That's devil talk! If you did wrong, ask God to forgive you and put it under the blood of Jesus. If you made a mistake—you didn't move here, or move there, take that job or whatever it was—just say, "Lord I'm going to put it under the blood of Jesus! It is all there; I'm not going to let the devil rob me of my peace because of something in the past." Do you know that you cannot change the past? So give it to God!!

The second weapon the devil uses is also two words: *What if? What if* the pandemic never quits? *What if* I get cancer? *What if* my child dies? What if my spouse would die? *What if, what if, what if*—you can go ont forever with that. *That's* what the devil is trying to do. He's trying to tie you all up, to tie me all up. *If only*—that's the past! *What if*—that's the future! You understand that you cannot change the past, but you cannot control the future either! If someone could, the smart ones would never have let COVID-19 develop into the crisis that we endured during the pandemic. Quit letting the devil tie you up with *If only* and *What if*!

Here's a little story about *What if.* To be very transparent, a few years ago I noticed blood in my urine. Everyone knows that's not good. After going to my doctor and then on to a urologist, I learned that I had a cancerous tumor in my bladder. The urologist explained, "This is serious." Surgery was scheduled to remove the tumor, but the *What ifs* started up in my mind: "*What if* the cancer is beyond the bladder? *What if* he must remove my bladder? *What if* I can't be traveling and preaching anymore because of complications?" I want you to know that I'm a sanctified, Spirit-filled Christian . . . but the *What ifs* kept coming anyway. (Sometimes we forget that we're still human.)

Now let's jump to today to let you know that over four years four cancerous tumors have been removed from my bladder. As of now I'm still feeling fine, my energy is still running strong, and God keeps opening doors for my preaching ministry. In fact, I'm preaching more than when I was a pastor! All of that is to say, "God is bigger than the *What ifs.*" God didn't remove the tumors . . . but He touched me in such a way that I haven't missed one preaching assignment because of bladder trouble during these recent years. Let me say it again: *God is bigger than the* What ifs *and the* If onlys. Don't let Satan tie you up in your mind or in your heart with those words. I've said it before and I'll say it again: *God is bigger!*

Do you know what I learned? When you get to the *What if,* God will be there too! Not everything always works out wonderfully well. Someday I'll die like everybody else, but in the case I just described, God provided! *If only* and *What if*—those are two of the weapons the devil uses to steal our peace, our joy, our blessings!

Quit saying *If only* and *What if.* Give it to God. The Lord is still in control, and when you get to the *What if,* God will be there and He'll get you through! Praise God! You need that! I need that today in more ways than you know, and somebody you know needs that, so share this with that person and tell him or her to take a few minutes to read this and he or she will learn two phrases to quit using. When we use those, we're letting the devil captivate our minds.

Let's rejoice that God is the God who can forgive your past and will control your future!

For that I praise the Lord! Rest in the promises of God and rejoice today because you have victory over the *If onlys* and the *What ifs.*" That's worth a *hallelujah!*

29 IF YOU CAN'T CHANGE IT, COMMIT IT TO CHRIST

Philippians 1

I want to give you a truth from the Scripture and then give you a story to illustrate that truth. Let's go right to Philippians 1. Paul, the leader of the early church in every way, was in a Roman prison for two years chained down, not able to do what God had called him to do, and yet he picked up his pen or pencil, or whatever they wrote with back then, and in essence said that God can bring good out of bad. That is another chapter. Let me go on in his letter here to tell you what he said next: "Some indeed preach Christ"—he's talking about preachers outside of the prison who were preaching Jesus—"even from envy and strife" (v. 15). That's not right! "And some also from goodwill: the former preach Christ from selfish ambition"—that's not right!—"not sincerely" (v. 16). They weren't even sincere in what they were doing, what they were saying. It's what you call being a hypocrite. That's not right! "Supposing to add affliction to my chains" (v. 16). *They know that I, Paul, am responsible, and I need to get out of this prison to go discipline them or remove them, but the motives of some of them are altogether wrong—envy and strife and some are preaching for whatever they can get out of it for themselves, for selfish ambition.*

Here's the point: "What then?" (v. 18). I don't know that Paul put his hands up, but I think so. *What can I do about it? I'm responsible, but I can't get out of here.* "What then? Only that in every way, whether in pretense or in truth, Christ is preached; and in this I rejoice, yes, and will rejoice" (v. 18).

Okay, Paul—what are you saying? How does it translate to the 2020s? Here's what it says to me: *If you can't change it, commit it to Christ.* Paul couldn't change the problem and go out and straighten out these preachers who did not have the right motives and the right spirit. So since he couldn't change it, he said, "I'll give them to you, Lord, and I will rejoice that God will take care of it." Oh, my—what a truth that we need today!

If you can change your situation, well, change it—but there are so many things we can't change. Have you lived long enough to learn there are more things in life you *can't* change than what you *can* change? You may have family members who are on the wrong track, and the more you try to change them, the more they resist. What are you going to do? Commit them to Christ! Commit them to Christ every day! You may have a marriage situation—commit it to Christ. You may have a financial situation or a physical situation. You may have scars from the past, abusive things that have happened to you, and it works on you and eats on you, but you can't go back and change it. Commit it to Christ! Give it to God and let God take care of it. Do you know God is bigger than we are? *God can do what we can't do!*

Once I had a preaching engagement at a rather large, very important event in Seattle. A friend picked me up and we were on our way to Denver International Airport, and as sure as the world, we got into one big traffic jam. I had to be in Seattle that night to kick off this event. We got to the airport late, and I got through all the check-in, went down and got on the train, made it to United Airlines at Concourse B, and went running down the concourse. My time was just about gone. I got to the gate, looked out the window, and thank the dear Lord, the plane headed to Seattle was still there. I rushed up to the gate agent and said, "I'm sorry I'm late, but I've got to get on the plane."

She looked at me and said, "No, sir. We've closed the door and the jet bridge has been pulled back. You can't go. You'll have to take the next flight."

The next flight would be so late that I would have missed the entire event in Seattle. I said, "I've *got* to be there," and she just replied, "I'm really sorry."

I stepped back a bit, and all I could pray was "Lord, if you want me in Seattle tonight, you've got to get me there. I can't do it!"

I hope you believe me—the phone then rang there at the counter, the agent picked it up, and she was listening to somebody. Then she hung the phone up, looked at me, and said, "You must be living right."

I said, "How come?"

She replied, "There's a man on the plane who's going to San Jose and he wants off. He's on the wrong plane. When we pull the jet bridge back and he comes off, you're going on, and you sit wherever he sat.

I said, "Are you kidding me?" She shook her head and said some other things like "This never happens" and so forth.

They got the thing done, the man came off the plane, I headed toward the plane, and he looked at me as we passed with a sly smile. I got on the plane, arrived in Seattle, preached that night, and we had a wonderful, wonderful service. My whole point is this: *I couldn't do it.* I couldn't open a door and say, "I'm going on this plane." I wanted you to know about this amazing instance in which God answered prayer instantaneously. Now, how that man ever got on that plane to Seattle with a ticket to San Jose, I'll never know. I'm telling you the truth—that's what happened!

Only God knows how all that was all put together. Sometimes He answers prayer like that, as when He healed the blind man and all of a sudden the man could see. Or when He brought Lazarus up from the grave and all of a sudden Lazarus was alive. But more often we give it to God, and then it's a process of time in which God brings it around to the way it ought to be. So I want to urge you today to believe that God can bring good out of bad. If you can't change it, commit it to Christ. He's bigger than you are! He's God! He can open an airplane door when I can't, and all I can say is "Thank you, Jesus," and that can be applied a thousand times over.

Whatever it is that's being brought to your mind now, commit it to Christ. Give Him time and He can bring it around so that you can rejoice!

God bless you, and thank the Lord—*God is in control.*

30 WHO CAN YOU TRUST ANYMORE?

Psalms 36:7; 37:3

Two out of the last three nights I've awakened about 4:00 a.m. I think that's too early. However, I believe the Lord has awakened me and for some reason it just seems that I'm hearing, "Trust, trust—who can you trust? Can people trust you?" I haven't been reading a lot along that line so I'm not sure what the Lord is trying to say, but I think I've got enough of it to give to you what I feel He has tried communicating to me.

Back a few years ago my mother-in-law, Gladys Stanley, who was living in Iowa, was hitting ninety years of age. She was starting to get forgetful, and different things were happening that evidenced her forgetfulness. We got a phone call: "Better come and get your mom. She's doing things you wouldn't be too happy about." We went to Oskaloosa, Iowa, rented a big U-Haul truck, and started loading up all of Mom's things. We were going to bring her back to Denver to live with us for a while, and then she would go on to assisted living. As we started loading things, I said, "Mom, where's the car?"

She said, "What car?"

I replied, "*Your* car. We gave you Dorothy's car, that red Pontiac. Don't you remember?"

"I don't remember. I don't remember," she responded.

Somebody apparently got into her life and fast-talked her into giving him or her the keys, and now the car was gone. It's still the joke around the Diehl family whenever we're together: "Who got Grandma's car?" We may never know, but I remember saying, "You can't trust anybody—they would take a car, steal a car, from a precious ninety-year-old grandma!"

Two nights ago after 8:00 my phone rang. It was a man with his rehearsed speech about the firefighters. "You're going to stand by them, aren't you? We've got a firefighters' fund and we want to know, sir, if you will help us with it." I didn't get the name of his group or his name—he talked too fast. I finally told him that if he would send me the literature, I would consider it and then send a check if I felt so led. Just like that, he switched me to somebody else, who was a little faster in his talk. This person said he wanted to save me time and money in the process, so he asked which credit card I would like to use. I guess he thought he would save me the time of writing a check and paying to put a stamp on the envelope.

I said to him, "What credit card? I don't even know your group. I don't know your name, and I've never heard of Grenada, Colorado, in my life. (That was what was on the caller ID.) I'm not giving you a credit card number. How crazy do you think I am?"

Click—he was gone! I said out loud, "Another scam. You can't trust anybody anymore."

Then in the mail two days ago came the election ballot. I believe in voting, and I'm going to vote, but I can't help but think and wonder, *Who can I trust?* Whoever I can trust is the one I will vote for.

Here's what I want to say today. I want you to know that there are still people in this world you can trust! I have people in my life whom I would trust with my checkbook. I would trust them with my safety deposit box key at the bank. I would trust them with the key to my house. I would trust them with my wife and family! There are people in my life, and I hope in your life too, whom you can trust.

Not everybody has broken our trust and I don't want to infer that. I do want to say, however, that I hope you can trust me, because if people don't trust me, I might as well quit talking and writing. I believe Christians are people you can trust! By the way, it starts in the Old Testament and goes all the way through the New—those who trust God are the ones who are going to heaven.

I decided to take one page in the Old Testament where trust is on both sides of the page. Psalms 36:7—"How precious is Your lovingkindness, O God! Therefore the children of men put their trust under the shadow of Your wings." Your wings! There's that theme again that I've used before—under the wings and the feathers of God. You can trust God!

Across the page is Psalm 37, a different psalm and possibly a different writer. This is what the writer said in verses 1–3: "Do not fret because of evildoers, nor be envious of the workers of iniquity. For they shall soon be cut down like the grass, and wither as the green herb. Trust in the Lord, and do good; dwell in the land, and feed on His faithfulness."

I want you to read carefully what I say today. In a world where you can't trust too many people (they'll steal your car or they'll steal your money in the dark of the night if you give out your credit card details over the phone), there are still trustworthy people! And you can trust God! You *can* trust God! You can trust God with your family, your finances, your job, your various situations, your health—*you can trust God!* He doesn't always give you what you want in your prayers, but He will give you what is right!

Three Hebrew young men in the Old Testament—Shadrack, Meshach and Abednego—were ordered, "Bow down to the golden image or you're burning in the fire."

"They didn't bend, they didn't bow, and they didn't burn!" God went into the fire with them. They were in the fire, but they trusted God and came *out* of the fire!

My mind is just swirling about other people who have tried to take me across the years, but I've decided to quit watching them and saying, '"You can't trust anybody." You *can* trust God and you *can* trust genuine, Christlike people!

I hope you can trust me, and in turn I will trust you and love you! Pass it on and God bless you! We're going to make it through because God won't fail you! Praise God for God and His people!

31 FEED THEM FAITH

Nehemiah 3–4

I woke up too early again a few mornings ago, around 4:30 again, and started praying about this time with you and what I needed to talk about with you. I prayed, *Lord, what do you want for this time? Which direction do you want me to go?* After a while I felt led to Nehemiah and what happened there. We will be in Nehemiah for the next few chapters—not the whole story, because entire books are written on Nehemiah's leadership in times of crisis. I'll take just one part of it this time.

First of all, God called Nehemiah from King Artaxerxes's court to go back to Jerusalem to inspire the people to rebuild the walls of Jerusalem and repair the gates, which had been burned. So he went back to Jerusalem—he was not invited by the people to come back; rather, he was invited by God to provide that leadership.

Now we jump right into Nehemiah and read what he was saying to the people. I want you to get the feeling for how he was speaking to them. In Nehemiah 2:20 he said, "The God of heaven Himself will prosper us; therefore we His servants will arise and build." Can't you hear that? Nehemiah was a leader inspiring his people. In 4:14 he said, "Do not be afraid of them." He was referring to the crowd who was still around who had torn the walls down in the first place. "Remember the Lord, great and awesome, and fight for your brethren, your sons, your daughters, your wives, and your houses." There was the leader—inspiring his people.

Now verse 20—"Wherever you hear the sound of the trumpet, rally to us there." Get this now: "Our God will fight for us." What was he doing to the people of Jerusalem? He was *feeding them faith.* Again, "The God of heaven Himself will prosper us," "Do not be afraid of them. Remember the Lord, great and awesome," "Our God will fight for us." He was feeding them faith!

Do we ever need that today in this confused world, in our divided nation with countless political problems as well as marches that turn into riots—and on and on. We need people who will feed each another faith. We don't need anybody else to feed fear. We don't need anybody else to feed us more doubts. We don't need anybody to feed us more wild ideas of being taken over by the aliens! We need people like you and me to feed each other faith.

Pastors, feed your congregation faith. They need it. They need to go home with one more kernel of truth and faith. God is still alive. God will fight for us. Come on—God is still in control! Moms and dads, feed your children faith; feed your grandchildren faith! Where do you get it? There's a whole load of promises in the Word of God, but feed your children and grandchildren stories of God's answers to prayer. In your life when something happens and God helps you, tell the family and maybe they'll remember it and recount that story at your funeral.

Friends, feed each other faith. Coaches, feed those athletes faith. Leaders, bosses, employers, feed your people faith! You can do it with a sticky note and put it on the mirror in the bathroom, the dash of the car, or maybe the backpack of your children as they head off to school. Maybe you can make a phone call—or a hundred other ways to feed faith.

Who fed me faith way back when I was just in my early years as a pastor? I started thinking about that and went through my library. I'm certainly not going to read books to you, but the first book that caused me to start thinking bigger than before was *Life Is Tremendous,* by Charlie Jones. Norman Vincent Peale—I tell you, he'll stir you up. Another one that really helped me was Zig Ziglar's *See You at the Top.* He helped me to think bigger than I had ever thought before. And then there's Robert Schuler's *Believe in the God Who Believes in You.* I mean, that brother would really feed you faith. Although those definitely have left a mark on me, there are of course other books like that from more current writers.

I want to tell you about a lady many of you would not know. Her name is Kathy Tate, and she used to live here in Denver with her husband, John, and they were part of our church where I was the pastor, Denver First Church of the Nazarene. Something happened in our lives (Dorothy and me), and she started sending cards to Dorothy with one promise on the back of each. They came each week for quite some time. The Tates eventually moved to Missouri, and these cards continued coming every week. I eventually called Kathy and told her that I loved these cards that she was sending Dorothy because I read them too.

Here's one: "Dear Dorothy, Do not lose heart. Prayers, Kathy." That's all it said. The next one: "Dear Dorothy, We have this hope as an anchor for the soul, firm and secure. Prayers, Kathy." Here's another: "Because the hand of the Lord my God was on me, I took courage," then the scripture and "Prayers, Kathy."

I said, "Kathy, I can't remember when you ever started this. How long have you been doing this for my wife, Dorothy?"

She said, "It was 1993 when that certain thing happened to you and I started sending your wife cards." She started feeding Dorothy promises in 1993 and continued doing it for over a quarter of a century. Folks, that's what I mean: *Feed them faith. Feed them faith!* These cards mean the world to me just because I know who was behind them.

You can do that now! You don't have to send everybody a card, but you can do as I was saying—by a phone call, an email, or some other way. By the way, I'm trying to feed you faith, but you feed *me* faith too by sending comments that really ignite my soul, so thank you!

Nehemiah said, "However, our God turned the curse into a blessing" (Nehemiah 13:2). If God did that in Nehemiah's day, He can do that today in your life, my life. "However, our God turned the curse into a blessing."

You need that! I need that! Share that with somebody. Feed that person faith. That's what the Lord whispered to me at 4:30 in the morning. God bless you. Let's do it—*feed them faith!*

32 PRAY, WARN, FEED FAITH, BACK TO WORK

Nehemiah 4

Previously I shared about two weapons Satan uses against us—*if only* and *what if*—and how he will try to steal our peace with these and other questions. In the last chapter I went to Nehemiah and picked out that truth there about the leader who fed the people faith. Many of you responded in turn by feeding *me* faith. In all your many words of encouragement and response, you fed me faith and I appreciate that very much.

I feel that the Lord wants me to go back to Nehemiah, because there's a whole lot more. Jerusalem, the holy city, the capital city of the Jewish nation, suffered from its walls having been torn down and lying in piles of rubble. The gates had been burned. The people were about as torn down as the walls because they did nothing to rebuild them. The walls were a reproach to all who walked by. God called Nehemiah from King Artaxerxes's court, 125 miles away, to leave all the royalty of the court to come to Jerusalem and inspire those people to get up, get going, and rebuild the walls!

However, those who had torn down the walls were still around. They hadn't disappeared, so it was not easy. But now the people were inspired because Nehemiah got them all organized. Each family had an assignment working on the wall. Of course, the devil tried to stop the work, and that is no different from today. As the scripture says, "We built the wall" (Nehemiah 4:6). When they were about halfway done, Sanballat, the leader of the enemy group, became very angry. He got all the opponents and conspired to attack Jerusalem and create confusion. That's another tactic or weapon of the devil—to create confusion. Does that ever picture us today?

I think of Denver, where I live, and all the tug-of-wars going on between this, that, and the other faction. Think of all the confusion going on now in Washington, DC. It's all around the world everywhere. Confusion, confusion—create confusion. We see that it's what the enemies in Nehemiah 4:8 tried to create, and that certainly is a picture of us and our world these days.

There's one more thing here. Judah, one of the good guys (of the Jewish or Jerusalem men), said, "The strength of the laborers is failing, and there is so much rubbish that we are not able to build the wall" (Nehemiah 4:10). In other words he was saying, "Nehemiah, my old buddy—we can't do it. This is worse than we ever thought. There's so much rubbish that we can't do it. Let's quit."

That is one of the greatest paragraphs in the Bible, picturing old-fashioned discouragement, creating confusion, and bringing on discouragement! Now, doesn't that picture our day—confusion, discouragement, and so on? What did Nehemiah do?

Number one, he called the people to prayer. As the scripture says, "Nevertheless we made our prayer to our God" (Nehemiah 4:9). That works today!

Number two: "Because of them we set a watch against them day and night" (v. 9). *We are not going to let Sanballat stop us! Don't get distracted by him. We're going to put trumpeters on the edge of where the city walls are, and if they come, they're going to blow the trumpets and we're all going to go there to fight. We are not going to let Sanballat defeat us!* Nehemiah said it strongly: *We're* not *going to let this defeat us!*

Number three: "Do not be afraid of them. Remember the Lord, great and awesome, and fight for your brethren, your sons, your daughters, your wives, and your houses" (v. 14). That is feeding faith!

Then number four: "All of us returned to the wall, everyone to his work" (v. 15). They all went back to work. It was quite a job, but it was done. It was completed, and the story is wonderful!

I want you to take those four things in today. How do we get through the situation we're in? Whether it is a pandemic or a storm in our lives, we will make it with these four things. Number one, *go to prayer* and get somebody to pray with you about it. Number two, decide that *we're not going to let any situation destroy* us. God is greater. God is bigger! Number three, *We have to feed each other faith.* Number four, *We get back to work.* The preachers need to preach, the teachers need to teach, the singers need to sing, and in the church world anyway, all the workers, youth, children, and others need to do what they do. To the rest of the people everywhere we do what we do—we make our phone calls, we drop our notes, and we feed each other faith.

One time early in my pastorate at Denver First Church when we were trying so hard to "rebuild the walls," we were hit with a major lawsuit that was going to kill us. I don't have time to get into all of that, but I definitely followed Nehemiah's lead. I called the people to prayer. We were not going to let this lawsuit divide us. I tried feeding them faith, and we went back to work. God brought a miracle, and instead of the church being ruined, the congregation actually grew.

Well, God bless you! You believe that God knows what He is doing? Four things:

1. Go to prayer,
2. decide that we're not going to let this stop us,
3. feed them faith, and
4. get back to work.

God bless you. Don't you dare quit! God is bigger. God is greater!

33 FAITHFULNESS OF GOD, GODLY LEADERS, GODLY LAYPEOPLE

Nehemiah 12

As you know, these were originally videos that we put out during the pandemic, and you've read where I said that those who watched the videos kind of became my "church." I heard from many, many, many every week, which really helps me know that I was not just speaking into the wind somewhere. Those were part of my virtual "church." Now you who are reading this are part of my "congregation" as well. Come on in, take a seat, and here we go.

If you have been reading, you know I've been in the book of Nehemiah in the Old Testament. The great leader whom God raised up, Nehemiah, was helping to inspire the Jewish people to rebuild the walls of the holy city. We will conclude our look at Nehemiah by noting all those who had a part in what happened with the rebuilding of Jerusalem.

I feel today that I would like to jump in at the end of the Nehemiah. The people were having a celebration, the dedication of the new wall, and they had thanksgiving choirs. It even tells us who the leaders of the choirs were, and do let me pick out a verse here: "The singers sang loudly with Jezrahiah the director" (Nehemiah 12:42).

They were having a time—their city was not a reproach anymore, the walls had been rebuilt, the gates had been repaired, they were no longer a disgrace, they were happy, they were filled with joy. "That day they offered great sacrifices, and rejoiced, for God had made them rejoice with great joy; the women and the children also rejoiced, so that the joy of Jerusalem was heard afar off" (v. 43). They were singing, the trumpeters were playing, everybody with an instrument was playing, and the joy of Jerusalem was heard afar off.

Here's my question for today: Why were they so happy? Why were they rejoicing so? Why were they singing at the top of their lungs? And why were people hearing them clear down in the valley and up on the other side of the ridges? Why were they so blessed? I think I know the answer. It's simple although profound.

Primarily *they rejoiced because of the faithfulness of God.* Back earlier it was noted in Scripture that after the wall was built, Sanballat said that they could not have done this without their God! Even the leader of the enemy forces said, "You couldn't have done that without God helping you!"

I want to tell you today, during all the confusion that all of us are facing, God is still helping us, and we ought to stop and say, "Thank God! I'm not trying to get through this confusing life all by myself. God is helping me!" As the little boy said when he knelt to pray, "Thank God for God!" With all respect to God, God didn't rebuild those walls or He would have done it earlier. Not one stone was put on top of another until Nehemiah heard the call of God, left his duties at King Artaxerxes's court, and came sacrificially to lead these people to rebuild the walls. *Thank God for God!*

Thank God for godly leaders like Nehemiah! But with all respect for Nehemiah, he didn't build the wall either—he led the people, he inspired them, he fed them faith, he helped them in every way he could. Thank God for the spiritual leaders in your life! I've been very pleased with how many pastors have written to me. So many of you have said, "Hey—I've preached from Nehemiah. Man, there's truth in there! Thanks for that." I want to tell you pastors—God bless you! You are spiritual leaders. Not everybody comes every week and hugs your neck, but I want to say thank God for our godly leaders! God was faithful, the leader Nehemiah was faithful, but as I said, he didn't build the wall.

Thank God for godly men and women who totally obeyed the call and put stone upon stone, fought against the enemy, stayed at it until they got the wall built. I say today, *Thank God for God.* Thank God for godly leaders whom all of us have had. But thank God also for those we call laypeople. These are the people in the pews, people who love God, who are faithful Christians. We can't see the kingdom grow without faithful people like you and like those in my life.

In one of my pastorates a certain fellow had become the "church boss." I can't get into the details of the situation, but it was becoming a burden on this pastor's mind and heart. After a certain board meeting I went back to the pastor's office, where one of the board members was waiting for me. He said, "You aren't going to stay with us very long, are you? I can tell this situation is wearing you down." After we talked a few minutes, he asked me out of the blue, "Do you take a shower every day?"

I laughed and said a strong "Yes! What's that got to do with this?"

His response was "I've got an idea. Every morning while you're taking your shower, pray for God to resolve this years-old situation. While I'm taking a shower across town, I'll be praying the same thing." We made a vow to each other that night that we would start "shower praying" for God to resolve the problem. He would ask me every Sunday if I was still faithful to "shower praying." I certainly was.

I can't go into detail here, but in a month or so the "church boss" came to me and said he was dealing with some mysterious physical problem and needed to resign his positions at the church. I kept a straight face, but inside I was doing a "hallelujah dance"! He resigned his positions but kept attending services. Through it all he really "mellowed out." His attitude changed. His conversations changed. His "threats" stopped.

Now years later, I can tell you that I believe God brought on that "mysterious illness."

God humbled his heart, and that man became my good friend. After some years he even came to see me in another state and thanked me for being a "dominant spiritual influence" in his life. Plus . . . the church healed and became healthy again.

What's my point? Thank God for godly laypeople like my friend who challenged me to do "shower praying." Thank God for God's faithfulness, for godly leaders, and for godly laypeople. It took all three to get the wall rebuilt. It was true in Nehemiah's day and it's still true today! Thank God!

34 SOMEONE IS TRYING TO STEAL YOUR JOY!

John 15:11; 1 John 1:4

Good day to you. The Scriptures tell us that the fruit of the Spirit comes from the Holy Spirit within our hearts as born-again, Spirit-filled Christians. The Bible says the fruit of the Spirit is love, joy, peace, and six more, but I don't want to mention all those nine evidences of the Spirit because that's the basis for about nine different messages.

I want to focus on one today: *joy.* The fruit of the spirit is joy! This is no surprise to you, but *someone is out to steal your joy.* Maybe we ought to put that into the plural—some *ones* or some *things* are out to steal your joy. Jesus wants you to be filled with His joy.

Let's go way back for a quick illustration. One of my first pastorates was in the great state of Iowa. I had been out that afternoon doing the work of a pastor or shepherd, going here and there visiting people in their homes. I also suppose that probably I had been to a nursing home or two to visit some of my elderly folks. I was just busy doing what God had called me to do and was on my way home as it was heading toward 5:00. Driving through a small subdivision, I saw one of the members of our church standing in his front yard watering his shrubs. I stopped and went up and greeted him, but he was of the negative sort—a murmurer, a complainer, and he was growling about something that I don't even remember. He was not happy, and then he said something to me that really cut my heart. I just knew I simply needed to say, "Hey—I'll see you later," and get going—so I did so.

I got into my car, irritated and aggravated. I was upset after spending all afternoon trying to help people and then getting cut in two at the last stop. I can remember saying, "Lord, I'm tired of this. What in the world? I try helping everybody—and the last one just kicks me."

I was going around a curve toward home, and if God the Holy Spirit ever spoke to me, He spoke to me in that Chevy at that curve: "How long are you going to let your joy be dependent on how he acts?" That was the Lord speaking into my mind. I pulled into the drive, put the car in park, turned the motor off, and I said, "Lord, I'm going to try it. I'm going to try to rejoice right now before I ever go into the house." I was the only one in the car, and out loud I said, "Thank you, Jesus. At least *you* love me, Lord! Thank you, Jesus, that *you* don't chew me out." I thought of something that has had me smiling many times since: "Thank you, Jesus—I'm glad I'm not married to him!" I had to think of something to be thankful for, but at that moment the Lord was teaching me a lifetime lesson. *How long are you going to let your joy be dependent on what he said, what she said, what they did, what has happened?*

What do we do with that? We must commit that boss, teacher, neighbor, maybe a church member, a person at the store, the one who said something to you he or she shouldn't have said. *Give that person to God!* If you can't change the situation, commit it to Christ! You can't go change all the people who are hurtful and cutting in what they do and say. You can't change them—*but* you can commit them to Christ!

John, who wrote those five books in the New Testament, is here now quoting Jesus: "These things I have spoken to you, that My joy may remain in you, and that your joy may be full" (John 15:11). That was Jesus! He wants you to have inner, deep joy. I'm not talking about just being happy, happy, happy. I'm talking about something a whole lot deeper—the joy of the Lord!

I looked up other scriptures on joy and this is the first time I ever put these two together in my understanding or thinking. First John 1:4 says, "These things we write to you that your joy may be full." These two exact phrases are there in these two important scriptures (John 15:11 and 1 John 1:4)—"that your joy may be full." I just really felt led today to ask you, *How is your joy?* The fruit of the Spirit is love, joy, and peace!

Satan wants to steal your joy, and usually it's through people. Some are good people, but some are dark—I think the devil's in their hearts. Don't let them steal your joy! Commit it or them to Christ!

There's one more thing I need to tell you. By the way, no matter how righteous you are, how Spirit-filled you are, it still hurts to get hurt, because we're still human! Don't tell me you can get so spiritual that people can't hurt you, lie to you or about you, or say things they shouldn't, and you say, "Oh, it's okay. God bless you." Are you kidding? It hurts, it hurts, it wounds because we're human. That's why we need to give it to God! Give that person, those persons, of the situation to God. Just remember this: part of the fruit of the Spirit is joy! Satan wants to steal your joy. Don't let him do it! Don't let him rob you! Take your joy back!

God will renew the joy of your heart no matter what he did, no matter what she did, no matter what they did, no matter what the devil would use to irritate you. I had a friend who used to say, "They know how to sandpaper you, don't they?" That is the personality of some people—they just "sandpaper" you! Don't let them steal your joy! Give them to God, let God deal with them, and you and the Lord can rejoice in your salvation.

We need to resist the devil and give to the Lord those who are stealing our joy. Claim the joy of Jesus and live in victory! Praise God! Have a good week and don't let anybody steal anything from you!

35 TRUSTING GOD WHILE GOING THROUGH A TUNNEL

Isaiah 26:3–4

Today we are continuing along the line of God saying to you and me, "Trust me! Trust me!" A few months ago I found a tremendous quote from Corrie ten Boom (shared in a previous chapter) that came out of her World War II experiences, which I'm sure many of you know about. This is what she wrote: "When a train goes through a tunnel and it gets dark, you don't throw away your ticket and jump off the train. You sit still and trust the engineer!" That's good!

I've had countless experiences in my life of going through tunnels, dark times. This story takes a little while to tell, but I'll make It brief. I was the district superintendent of the Church of the Nazarene in Nebraska. I had been there five years and moving into year six. This impression started coming to me: *You won't be here a year from now. This is your last year.* I believed that was an impression from God, but I didn't tell anyone except my wife.

"Dorothy, I don't think we'll be here next year."

She asked "Well, where are we going?"

"Only God knows. I don't know. Don't tell anybody because I'm going to give it my best here until the last day."

On May 23, 1985, I was at the wedding of Dave, our son, and Lori at College Church of the Nazarene in Olathe, Kansas. I officiated, and when the wonderful ceremony was finished, I followed the wedding party out of the sanctuary. Someone grabbed me by the arm, pulled me aside, and said, "Here's a telephone number. There's a general superintendent after you and he wants you to call him now!"

I said to Dorothy, "Go ahead to the reception. I'll catch up to you in a minute." I went down the end of a long hall and called Dr. Jerry Johnson.

Dr. Johnson said, "You were just elected district superintendent today in Arizona. I would love to tell them tomorrow in our session, which goes until noon, to let them know you accepted. Are you ready to say yes?"

I said, "What? I didn't even know you were having district assembly. I haven't prayed a prayer about this. I'm at our son's wedding. I've got to get on into the reception. No, I can't say yes now for this huge responsibility."

He said, "I didn't know you were in all of that. Take your time and call me Monday. Calm down—don't worry about it."

I went into the reception, and Dorothy asked, "Who was that?"

I said, "We were just elected DS today in Arizona."

She responded, "Oh, so that's where we're going?"

The next day we went back to Hastings, Nebraska. I unloaded the car, left Dorothy there, got back in the car, and drove and drove, alone with God. "Lord, so this is it? You want us to go to Arizona? Well, it's a great district, about twice the size of Nebraska in membership, in churches, finances and everything. I guess it is quite the promotion, but I feel dead. I feel empty. I feel dark. Lord, if you want me to go there to Arizona, can't you let one joy bell ring in my heart?"

I drove on another forty or fifty miles. "Lord, I feel like I've been to a funeral or I'm going to one. Arizona is a wonderful district; they've got that great camp there in Pine Rock. I love that place in Prescott. Lord, please—is this where you want us to go?"

Silence, darkness, heaviness. By the time I got to Valentine, 233 miles from Hastings, I said, "All right, Lord. We've got to make a decision. I'm not going to Arizona. I don't understand this—you've prepared me for a year and now it's just all dark. I'm not going!" Calmness came. Peace came, and that was the decision! I didn't go to Arizona!

Then the devil came and started putting doubts in my mind. He tends to do that, especially at night. Have you noticed? "How about this? What are you going to do about that? How crazy can you get, Diehl? Don't you know a promotion when you see it? You've missed it now."

That was the last half of May, and then in late June at General Assembly in Anaheim, California, some friends came around and said, "Diehl, what's the matter with you? You got elected to one of the greatest districts—and you said no?"

I said, "I know. I know."

"What are you doing?"

"I'm just trying to mind God."

"Aww, come on. There has to be some other reason."

Then the devil jumped on me: "Okay, you've missed it, you've blown it. Even your friends are telling you that you blew your chance."

Halfway through July I said, "Lord, why did you prepare me and then came the offer—and then the answer was no?"

In mid-July the phone rang. Another general superintendent, Dr. Raymond Hurn, said, "Hey, Brother Diehl! You've just been elected district superintendent today in Colorado."

I said, "What?"

"You were elected today in Colorado!"

Ding! I felt a green light clicking on in my heart and mind. Ding! That's it! That's it! But I said, "I'll pray about it and call you tomorrow."

I think you know that we ended up going to Colorado. I have now had some years since then to say, "Lord, why did you prepare me and then you allowed Arizona to come? That was dangerous!"

I really believe the Lord whispered to me and said, "I wanted to see if you would take man's green light or wait for *my* green light." God's green light was Colorado. I look back on that now and recall that Denver First Church had a crisis after my first four years as Colorado District Superintendent, and they more or less drafted me to become their pastor. After the first year, which was the toughest of my life, God came on that church, and we actually ran 1,900-plus in attendance. Then four years later I was elected as general superintendent, and I travelled all over the country and around the world for sixteen years. That's a whole other story, but I look back on that and remember the scripture that was ringing in my ears: "You [God] will keep him in perfect peace, whose mind is stayed on You, because he trusts in You. Trust in the Lord forever" (Isaiah 26:3–4).

I feel so strongly that a lot of you need to read this today. Trust in the Lord—He will keep you in perfect peace! Even though conflicting things come: Trust in the Lord!

The Lord whispered to me one day, "I had it all worked out for you. I'm glad you didn't say yes to man's green light; you waited for *my* green light!" Trust in the Lord—He will keep you in perfect peace!

Remember—when you are in a dark tunnel, you don't jump off the train. You trust the engineer!

36 WE REALLY DO NEED EACH OTHER

Ecclesiastes 4:9–12; Matthew 5:16

One Saturday morning not long ago I was working outside our home and wondered about the gutters and downspouts. They get filled with leaves and pine straw through the winter. I have a sixteen-foot metal ladder that folds out four times and I finally got that thing all stretched out. I wrestled with the ladder and finally got it extended up to the roof to where I could scamper up there. Just then a neighbor, Gary, drove by and stopped. He hollered out, "What are you doing anyway?"

I said, " Hi, Gary. I'm going to get up there and clean out these gutters."

He responded, "No, you're not. I'm going to do that." In a moment he was climbing up on our roof and thankfully saw that everything was good with that part of the gutters. He then hollered out, "What else?"

I said, "Let's go down to that corner of the house." So across the roof he went and found that those gutters were clear. He wanted to know if I wanted him to crawl around the roof and look at all of them.

I told him that was enough, so he came back down and we talked just a little while. Then he slapped me on the shoulder, said, "Behave yourself," and took off.

Gary helped me that Saturday, and since I'm a little over eighty years old, it's just a little safer to have a younger man help like that. Dr. Reuben Welch, a great writer, speaker, and professor at Point Loma Nazarene University, wrote a book titled *We Really Do Need Each Other,* and the words of that title echo in my head often. The more I have thought about it since that Saturday and the more I reflect on the pandemic and other reasons that so many people have become isolated and lonely, the more I believe we really do need each other.

I got to thinking about how God created Adam and said, "It is not good that man should be alone" (Genesis 2:18). He then made a helpmate for Adam and named her Eve. Adam and Eve soon had a family. That's God's plan. He doesn't want us to live alone. The writer of Ecclesiastes wrote in chapter 4:8, "There is one alone, without companion: He has neither son nor brother. Yet there is no end to all his labors." In other words, he works all the time and there is no satisfaction with riches. But now read this: "Two are better than one, Because they have a good reward for their labor. For if they fall, one will lift up his companion. . . . If two lie down together, they will keep warm" (Ecclesiastes 4:10–11). Then verse 12: "Though one may be overpowered by another, two can withstand him. And a threefold cord is not quickly broken." I have written on the edge of that page in my Bible, "We are better together."

I want to ask you today—will you reach out to somebody? There are lonely elderly people, lonely widows and widowers, lonely single adults, and others who are lonely because of the various circumstances of life. The Lord Jesus said we are to our love our neighbors, and that means to love them in more than simply words. We need to add *action* to our words.

I have talked a lot about the "five-minute ministry" across the years. It only takes five minutes to make an encouraging phone call, five minutes to send a text, five minutes to stop and chat with a neighbor, five minutes to encourage a friend.

You may not believe this, but while I was writing this, the phone rang, and it was Kerm Kidder from Florida. He said, "I'm on the job but I had a few minutes, and you were on my mind."

He asked how Dorothy and I were doing. "I'm writing about this right now," I responded, "the five-minute ministry."

He replied, "I've got to go but I'm praying for you. I'll call you later."

It was just five minutes! His happy voice, his care for us, his promise of prayer support, his love—Kerm Kidder brightened my day.

You can do that. You can make a quick phone call. You can send a short text. You can have a brief chat with someone at the post office, the grocery store, or the gas station. If you will, remember what Reuben Welch said—"We really do need each other"—and when you reach out to someone today, you can be the voice of Jesus to that person.

Do it today! Truthfully, it will do you as much good as it does for the other person!

37 YOU CAN MAKE IT THROUGH TOUGH TIMES

2 Timothy 4:6–8

On the day that I'm writing this, Dorothy and I are here at our home in Lakewood, Colorado, where over the weekend we had the fourth-heaviest snowstorm on record. It was around twenty-seven to twenty-eight inches of snow, so everything out the windows is all white and beautiful. We have been through a year of the pandemic, which has affected all of us. Life was totally different in your life, my life, the life of the church, business, sports, school—everybody's life. Things were so different and difficult, with over a million deaths from COVID-19 across the United States.

So my mind started focusing on tough times. Who in the Bible could give us a little bit of inspiration concerning tough times?

My mind and heart were drawn to Paul and the letter he wrote to his spiritual son, Timothy (2 Timothy). Paul was in prison for the last time. The execution date had been set and it was now just days away. He had not committed a crime. He was not truly a criminal, but he was the leader of the people called Christians. Evidently the prison personnel had come to him in prison and said, 'Mr. Paul, whatever you're going to write, get it done because the day has come.

We're going to take you out since the execution site is ready."

I have written in my Bible at the top of the page in 2 Timothy, "Last Words from Death Row." That's what this letter is, Paul's last words. He was facing death, he was soon to be a martyr, this was the end, and he knew it! Look at what he said in 4:6–7: "I am already being poured out as a drink offering, and the time of my departure is at hand. I have fought the good fight, I have finished the race, I have kept the faith."

That is tremendous, that is powerful, that is strong! The paragraph heading in the new King James Version is "Paul's Valedictory" or his farewell speech. He had finished the race, he had done what God wanted him to do, he had kept the faith, and now he was going home! He went on to say a few farewell words and then closed: "Goodbye, Timothy. I love you, my son. I'll see you over there!" The historical account tells us that Paul was taken out, his life was taken from him, and he went home to heaven. But he did not go out a victim—he went out a victor! He lived in victory and he died in blessing! He lived in tough times. So do we, but we can make it through tough times!

How in the world did Paul keep such a victorious spirit amid the threat and then the reality of death? I want to dig his own words from another letter, which was to the Philippians, where he wrote, "I can do all things through Christ who gives me strength" (4:13). *That's* the way he made it! That's the way *we* can make it! That's the way you can make it through your tough times! "I can do all things through Christ [underline it—<u>through Christ</u>] who gives me strength."

My friend, I just felt today that we've gone through some tough years. We're about worn out with it, we're ready for life to get back to some kind of normalcy, but I want you to know *you can make it!* You can make it, Mom or Dad. You can make it, businessperson.

You can make it, preacher, pastor friend. You can make it, teenager. You can make it not by gritting your teeth and saying, 'I'm going to make it," but by proclaiming, *I can do all things through Christ, who strengthens me.* That's the way we can make it! It is through the strength, the courage, the direction, and power of Jesus Christ the Lord within our hearts and lives!

None of us enjoy the tough times, but with the help of God may we say with the apostle Paul, "I have fought the good fight, I have finished the race, I have kept the faith. Finally, there is laid up for me the crown of righteousness, which the Lord, the righteous Judge, will give to me on that Day" (2 Timothy 4:7–8).

38 GOD TURNED THE CURSE INTO A BLESSING

Nehemiah 13:2; Deuteronomy 23:5

I found a scripture that you must read. It's Nehemiah 13:2: "However, our God turned the curse into a blessing." Briefly let me share with you the story behind this. The children of Israel were marching out of Egypt, all the way to the promised land, being led by Moses. Somewhere out there on that journey they were met by the Ammonites and the Moabites, and instead of giving bread and water to this great group of people who were trekking through the desert, they put a curse on them. This same account is also recorded in Deuteronomy 23:5: "Nevertheless the Lord your God would not listen to Balaam, but the Lord your God turned the curse into a blessing for you, because the Lord your God loves you." The part I want you to underline in your Bible is this: "The Lord your God turned the curse into a blessing for you, because the Lord your God loves you."

The more I've been thinking about it and praying about it, I'm reminded that many of you are dealing with the curse of cancer or the curse of heart trouble or the curse of something like Parkinson's disease, dementia, Alzheimer's disease, or an untimely death that has left you alone. It might be the curse of a broken relationship that still has you wounded or the curse of someone who has abused you and you're having a hard time dealing with the scars. That list can go as long as you want, but we need to get it off the pages of the Bible and into your life and mine. "However, our God turned the curse into a blessing." He did it for them and He's done it for me more times than I can count!

I thought of all the illustrations that would fit and felt led to use this one. We were going to our second pastorate, in Indianola, Iowa. We were all excited and had been told the church was somewhat larger than where we had been. While we were unloading the moving truck, one of the guys from the church helping us unload said, "Now you know, don't you, that we've had a split in the congregation? There's a bunch of people who aren't coming anymore, and our crowd is down."

I said," No, I didn't know that."

He said, "You need to know that we are a wounded church."

I told my wife, Dorothy, "You know, honey, I think we've come into a problem here. This church is broken. It's fractured."

She said, "I guess whatever it is—it's what it is. It's too late to back out now."

The next day (I think it was Friday) I got into the car to go down Main Street and then turned left on South Howard Street to go to the city square. My purpose was to open a checking account at the bank, but I remembered something that I needed to call my wife about. I took a right turn at South Howard Street, because in half a block there was the church, the Church of the Nazarene, where I could make the call. When I turned the car, it jumped, shook, and blew up, making sounds as if saying, "I can't even make it here today." I got out, looked, and noticed that the "blood" (oil) was running onto the street from the car. The car died and—I'm not joking—it never ran again. It went to the junkyard. I proceeded to the church, unlocked the door, went in, found the phone, and called my wife. "Guess what else is broken around here. Now we don't have a car."

She said, "Jim, I don't know what's going on, but evidently the washing machine wasn't hooked up right, and there's running water all over the floor. Get home and help me!"

I said, "I *can't* get home—I don't have a car." It was at least two miles from the church to the parsonage, and I don't know to this day if I walked or if somebody gave me a ride, but I finally got back home. The church was broken, the car was broken forever, and now the washing machine was broken. I was the most discouraged pastor in Iowa, and I hadn't even been there for a Sunday yet! We fell into bed that night, and I guess we hadn't put the slats into the frame right, because the mattress and foundation fell right down onto the floor. I said, "Let her go—let her go," and we slept on the mattress on the floor that night. You can't make this stuff up!

We had our first Sunday at the church. The crowd wasn't close to what I thought it was going to be. On Monday, the next day, the phone rang, and it was a little old lady I had never met who was a member of the church but couldn't attend anymore because of her age and situation. She said, "Pastor, come see me. I really want to see my new pastor and I've got something to talk to you about." I borrowed a car and went over to find her, and she said, "I hear we're in kind of a mess at the church."

I said, "Yes, I found that out too."

She said, " I've heard that we're three months behind on our mortgage payment."

I said, "Yes, I found that out yesterday as well."

"Well," she said, "I can't do much, but I can do a little." She went shuffling off to the bedroom and came back with a sock—I mean a sock like what you wear on your foot. That sock was stuffed with twenty-dollar bills. She said, "I can't do very much, but I'm going to pay one month's mortgage payment right now. We've got to get this church going again." She started peeling these twenty-dollar bills out onto a little coffee table and said, "I can't see very well—stop me when I get there."

All of a sudden I became as blind as a bat. "Go on. Keep peeling, lady—peel" That was the first good thing that had happened since I been in town! No, I actually stopped her at the right amount, and I hugged that precious lady and had prayer with her. You know what I did that next Sunday? I told the church about that elderly lady, I told about that money—I even had her money in my hand. I said to that congregation, "Come on, folks. What are you going to do? She paid for one month's mortgage payment. What can the rest of us do?"

The crowd responded, and in one month all past-due mortgage payments were paid plus all past-due bills. That church "caught fire" and grew from 55 on the first Sunday to 60, 70, 80, 90, 100, 110, to 120. Now that didn't happen in a week or two—it was over a few years— but it went from 55 to 120 in average attendance and became a very vibrant, lively, wonderful church. Now I look back and say, "God turned the curse into a blessing!"

I was thinking about this last night and wondered about what kind of a reward God gave that precious little lady when she went to heaven for the sacrifice she made, which actually inspired the entire church. The church was never the same after that. They took on new life!

"The Lord your God turned the curse into a blessing for you, because the Lord your God loves you" (Deuteronomy 23:5). Take that truth for yourself! Read that in your Bible and underline it in red and claim it for your situation. Share it with somebody else—because the Lord can indeed turn a curse into a blessing today—even for you. What a powerful truth for today! Praise God!

39 DON'T LIVE FOR THE TEMPORARY —LIVE FOR THE ETERNAL

James 4:14

When we did one of these podcasts, we had just come through a major election for president of the United States. It was contentious, high energy, and in many ways stirred up high anger levels. It was just not a good time for peaceful living, but Joe Biden had more votes than President Trump, so Joe Biden was elected president. That made many of you happy, but it made many others of you upset, I'm sure not going to get into all of that or I'll ruin my connection with you. What I'm trying to say is that all this focus on our president caused me to wonder how many presidents have been in office since I've been alive.

I have my little list here. Franklin D. Roosevelt was the president when I entered this great world. Then there was Harry Truman, Dwight Eisenhower, John F. Kennedy, Lyndon Johnson, Richard Nixon, Gerald Ford, Jimmy Carter, Ronald Reagan, George H. W. Bush, Bill Clinton, George W. Bush, Barack Obama, Donald Trump, and now Joe Biden That's fifteen in my lifetime so far. I thought about them and even checked on how long they served and learned that Franklin Roosevelt served the longest, a little over twelve years, and the shortest was John F. Kennedy, who had served just about a thousand days before being assassinated in November 1963.

I thought of some other similarities and very big differences among the fifteen men who have been president of the United States. Then a thought struck me: *All leadership is temporary!* Let that soak in for a moment. All these fifteen men who were president of the United States of America were there in that position, but none of them is there now except for Joe Biden! A few are still alive, but most have gone on to meet the Lord. Each of them was the most powerful person in the world for a few years. But for all the power, it didn't last too long—four years for some, eight years for some, one a bit longer, and a couple shorter, but then it's over and life goes on.

The more I think about that, the more profound it gets: *All leadership is temporary!* I got to thinking about me and my own leadership positions in churches and districts. In district leadership I was district superintendent over all the Nazarene churches in Nebraska, then over all the Nazarene churches in Colorado. Ultimately I was elected general superintendent of the denomination and was one of six who traveled around and around the world. My terms lasted for a total of sixteen years, but it was still temporary. I'm not there now. I don't do that anymore. That's all in the past.

All leadership is temporary, but then my mind goes to this thought: *All lives are temporary!* It is not just leadership—it's your life, my life, everybody we know. We're here only temporarily and then there's eternity, which will last forever! The Lord has certainly talked to us about that through various writers in Scripture.

Let me share with you this verse from James 4:14: "Whereas you do not know what will happen tomorrow. For what is your life? It is even a vapor that appears for a little time and then vanishes away." The Bible says our lives in the view of eternity are as long as a vapor. One translation says we're just a mist and gone; we are a puff of steam then gone. Another translation says we're a puff of smoke and we're gone.

I want you to consider today that this life is all that we know—but it's temporary! Therefore, what should we do with the one and only life we have? You've heard me say this before, but I'll say it again: First, *get totally right with God!* We are going to live forever in eternity, either with God in His bright heaven or with the devil in his outer darkness of hell! If we're going to exist forever, don't you think we had better get right with God now? Don't wait until you're on your deathbed. Get right with God *now!*

Number two, *invest your life in people!* Invest in the lives of children, teenagers, young adults, adults, a men's group, a women's group, a singles' group, and don't forget the senior adults! The older I get the more I think about them. *Invest your life in people!*

Don't live your life for the temporary—live your life for the eternal! That means not to live your life for just what comes, goes, and will pass away here, but rather live your life for the God who is forever! I was reading from James about our lives, which are so short, and then in Hebrews 13:8 we read, "Jesus Christ is the same yesterday, today, and forever." I am temporary, you are temporary—but Jesus is forever! He's God! God the Father, God the Son, God the Holy Spirit have an eternity for us, but you have to give your life to Him if you want to experience heaven forever.

You may or may not know that my videographer was my son-in-law, Bernie, who filmed the "Refuel" video sessions for this time together, which as you know is where this book originated. When we were recording this particular one, he came in that morning and told me that one of his dear lifetime friends had died the night before, another illustration that this life is so temporary. I have also lost many of my college mates and friends from pastorates and churches, people who were around the same age as me. Life is temporary, but eternity is forever!

So let's pray for our president—that's the right thing to do—but above all, put your focus on the Lord Jesus and Him forever! He will make this temporary life worthwhile. Yes, yes, yes—live for God, serve people, and forever will be wonderful! God bless you all.

40 JEHOVAH RAPHA: OUR HEALING GOD

Exodus 15:26; Matthew 4:23

During the time we were presenting these chapters as videos, there was a great deal of sickness with lots of COVID-19 cases plus other illnesses. I received many prayer requests for healing during that time. As I was praying for these people, it just seemed that the Lord impressed upon me to tell them and you that we serve not only a saving and sanctifying God but a healing God as well!

In the Old Testament a wonderful promise was given to the children of Israel in Exodus 15:26: "I am the Lord who heals you." He is Jehovah Rapha, the God who heals. That was the first announcement that God is a healing God. In the fullness of time Jesus came: "Jesus went about all Galilee, teaching in their synagogues, preaching the gospel of the kingdom, and healing all kinds of sickness and all kinds of disease among the people" (Matthew 4:23). Then to make sure we got the message, Matthew repeated it in 9:35: "Jesus went about all the cities and villages, teaching in their synagogues, preaching the gospel of the kingdom, and healing every sickness and every disease among the people."

People seem to be in great need of healing today, not only of diseases, but many have past wounds, hurts, or scars. They can be healed of those or delivered from addictions, bad habits, and more. Jesus is the healing God as well as the Old Testament Jehovah Rapha.

I want you to know that I have been healed. There's a very definite healing story in my life and it happened back in 1996. Something was wrong in my throat area and it was finally focused down to the thyroid. I had cancer of the thyroid and a Jewish doctor here in Littleton, Colorado, said to me, "You're going to have to sign a waiver before we do this surgery. You may not have a voice when I get done. Your voice may cut in and out or it may be gravelly for the rest of your life or you may talk in a whisper." He must have seen the look on my face—because if I'm a preacher and I'm going all over the world preaching (which I was at that time as a general superintendent in the Church of the Nazarene), how could I preach if I didn't have a voice? I think he read my body language, and I'm not making this up—this is what he said: "It's about time that you get 5,000 of those Nazarene friends of yours to pray for you because that's where you are."

I got the word out and I don't know how many prayed, but I think there was a prayer army. I had the surgery. It was four and a half hours long and there was no thyroid left. I had to wait about a month or so and then go back in for a second surgery. The first one was January 29, 1996. The second one was March 4, 1996. After that, I had to go through nuclear medicine and I was so radioactive that I was isolated in a hospital room for twenty-four hours. I couldn't see anybody or talk to anybody. After all of that, they did a full body scan, came in, and said, "There's no cancer anywhere. We don't see a shadow anywhere in your body."

I responded, "Praise God!"

I want you to know today that I honor the surgeon, Dr. Seth Riner, who is still in practice, but I believe with all my heart that the healing came from Jesus Christ, our Lord—Jehovah Rapha, "the

God who heals." Oh, by the way, I can still talk. Praise the Lord! I will never get over the truth that God healed me.

If I was near wherever you live, we would get together somewhere or I would come to your home and would bring the anointing oil, because the book of James indicates that we need to call for the elders of the church, or the spiritually mature ones, and anoint with oil, and the prayer of faith will save the sick. I can't come to where you are and anoint you and pray for your healing, but you can call in a friend or two and they can anoint you and pray for you.

Remember: the reason we anoint with oil is that James 5:14 instructs us to do that, and recall that oil is a symbol of the Holy Spirit. I can't heal you, the person who prays for you can't heal you, and the oil cannot heal you. It's a living Jesus who heals you! I know I'll die someday (unless Jesus comes first)—but I won't die because of thyroid cancer. God healed me of that in 1996. Praise God forever!

From the Old Testament "Jehovah Rapha" to the New Testament "Jesus the Healer," we serve a healing God! "And the prayer of faith will save the sick, and the Lord will raise him up" (James 5:15). We serve a saving God, a sanctifying God—and a healing God! Praise be to God! Let Him heal you today!

41 I'M THANKFUL FOR WHAT DIDN'T HAPPEN

Psalm 100

When I presented this sermonette on the podcast videos, it was Christmas month—but this is appropriate at any time. I want to mention various things we can thank God for, plus the coming of Jesus Christ the Lord. In that regard I feel drawn back to one of the classic psalms, Psalm 100. It's along the praise line. It doesn't say actually mention Christmas, but you'll pick up on that anyway:

> Make a joyful shout to the Lord, all you lands!
> Serve the Lord with gladness;
> Come before His presence with singing.
> Know that the Lord, He is God;
> It is He who has made us, and not we ourselves;
> We are His people and the sheep of His pasture.
> Enter into His gates with thanksgiving,
> And into His courts with praise.
> Be thankful to Him, and bless His name.
> For the Lord is good;
> His mercy is everlasting,
> And His truth endures to all generations.

That's a classic psalm, one that I really love, and it's still true today. Here is the story I want to tell you today. I'm thankful for what didn't happen.

Let's go to the Oklahoma City area, Bethany in particular. Our granddaughter Brooke and her husband, Trey Keoppel, live and work there. They have three children: Gracie, Kort, and Remi. Oklahoma had a record-setting ice storm. If you've never experienced an ice storm, it happens when the surface temperature is at freezing or below and the rain freezes on just about everything. Trees were breaking and falling, and power lines were out. In fact, power was out all over the metro area.

It was October 20, 2020, when this particular storm occurred. Brooke and Trey had no heat in their house and no electricity; they were using candles to see at nighttime. They finally went out and rented a generator, which was $100 a day, so you certainly don't want to do that very long. They brought the generator to the house around four in the afternoon, and the one thing that the salesperson who rented it to them said was "Don't let it get iced over." Therefore, they couldn't leave it outside. They took it into the garage and got the generator going to provide some electricity for the refrigerator and the freezer and possibly some lights. But not the furnace—the generator was not big enough to do all that. They sat down and ate the evening meal and then tried to get a little warmth from the fireplace.

Later in the evening Kort said that he couldn't keep awake so he was going to bed. Then they took little Remi (the baby), who was about two years old, and put her in bed. Then the rest of them were there for just a little while longer and finally they said, "We're all so tired and cold—let's just all go to bed." When they got up to go, their little dog, Hogan, started walking with them and Brooke said he walked as if he were drunk—and then he fell onto the floor.

Gracie went over to see what was wrong with the dog, and then she collapsed too. Then Trey came in to see what was going on and he wasn't making sense with whatever he said, and he fell on the floor.

Brooke realized something terrible was happening. How she got Trey, who's one big guy, out on the porch I don't know, but then they got Gracie out and then went back to get the other two. She said that when she picked up Remi, she seemed lifeless. She got her out on the porch, along with Kort, and then they called 911.

In a hurry the paramedics were there, plus fire trucks, and they came into the house to check the carbon monoxide, which pegged the top of the meter. I called her later to get it all straight. She told me about the carbon monoxide being so high that they were being gassed to death and didn't know it! The paramedics went to work on them and tried to air out the house while prohibiting them from going back into the house, warning Trey and Brooke that they could not stay there that night. They had to find a place to stay and ended up going to their church, Bethany First Church of the Nazarene, which gave them a room somewhere and they all bunked out there as in a youth camp, I guess.

The family lived through it. Brooke explained to me that when their little dog, Hogan, walked as if he were drunk and then collapsed, that started telling them that something was seriously wrong. "Hogan saved our lives," Brooke said. I believe that, but we all know that behind all of this God orchestrated what happened to save an entire family. One of the firemen said, "If you all had gone to bed and fallen to sleep, none of you would have awakened in the morning. Five people would have been killed by the carbon monoxide."

What's my point today? Thank God for what didn't happen! God intervened in what I just described and saved a dad, a mom, and three children. We are so thankful that God saved our granddaughter and her husband and our three great-grandkids! I surely thank

God that we didn't have a five-person funeral. I can't even imagine.

It brings me back to the Word of God: "Enter His gates with thanksgiving"—thank you, Lord—"and into His courts with praise." Praise God for helping them in that dreadful situation! "Be thankful to Him, and bless His name."

I want you to think now what the Lord has done to save *you* from tragedy. Thank Him again for what He did to keep something tragic from happening to you and your family.

Lord, we thank you, we praise you, and we bless your name from the things you have protected us from, even those we may not have realized.

As we get ready to celebrate Christmas, let's rejoice for recent answers to prayer! Jesus has been born and we can be connected to Christ the Lord in our hearts. I say, "Praise God today and bless His name—and God bless *you*!

42 GOD REWARDS FAITHFULNESS

Matthew 25:14

Jesus told a story in Matthew 25 starting with verse 14. He told a lot of stories, but read this: *For the kingdom of heaven is like . . .* He wasn't just spinning a tale; he was talking about the very kingdom of heaven, the kingdom of God, and this is one more illustration of how the kingdom of God works.

He told about a master who had servants, and the master gave to his servants—I like the way the New Century Version puts it: *He gave one servant five bags of gold* (v. 15)—now that helps us to see that he gave them something of value, money, and *another servant two bags of gold, and a third servant one bag of gold.* The master said, "I'll be gone. I want to give you this investment, and when I come back we will then see what you have done with the talent, the money, the abilities that I have given to you."

It's a story not just about money but also about our gifts, our graces, and our opportunities. Oh, I want you to hear that! Some people have great opportunities in life, some have very limited opportunities, and some have hardly any opportunities to really do something out of the ordinary.

The master was gone for some time. Then he came back and called for the servants to come and to give him a report. The one with five talents or five bags of gold said, "I've taken the five bags and have turned them into ten," because of his abilities and business abilities. "Now I have ten."

The master said, "You did well. You are a good and loyal servant. Because you were loyal with small things, I will let you care for much greater things. Come and share my joy with me" (v. 21).

The one who had two bags of gold came back and said, "I have taken the two and have invested here, there, and everywhere, and I now have four bags."

The master responded, "You did well. You are a good and loyal servant. Because you were loyal with small things, I will let you care for much greater things. Come and share my joy with me" (v. 23).

The one who received one bag of gold came and said, "I knew you were a tough, hard taskmaster, and I took that talent, that bag of gold, and hid it in the ground. I just finished digging it up. Here—this is what you gave me. I give it back to you."

The response to that was "You are a wicked and lazy servant! You say you knew that I harvest things I did not plant and that I gather crops where I did not sow any seed. So you should have put my gold in the bank. Then, when I came home, I would have received my gold back with interest. . . . Throw that useless servant outside, into the darkness where people will cry and grind their teeth with pain" (vv. 26–27, 30).

Just a couple of highlights here today that I want you to catch. The first one is this: we are all gifted differently. Some are five-talent people while some become ten-talent. Some are two; some are one. None of us has the same gifts, abilities, or opportunities. That's just not the way life works. Some have more, some have less. We are not the same with what has been given to us.

Truth number two for us is this: the two-talent servant, who grew his money into four talents (bags), received the exact same commendation as the five-talent servant, who developed his five talents (bags) into ten. It was not as if the five-talent servant heard, "Fantastic! Here—come on in—and the one with two bags heard, "Wonderful." No, no—it's not as if one got gold, one got silver, and one got bronze. That's not the kingdom of God.

Rather here's the point. Our Lord Jesus seems to put the emphasis on two things. Read this carefully now: "Well done, good and faithful servant!" God puts the emphasis on *good* and *faithful*! Only God can make you or me good! By the blood of Jesus Christ, which has been shed on the cross, our sins can be forgiven, Jesus can live in our hearts and lives, and we can be brand-new creations. God can make us good, but only we have the power of choice as to whether to be faithful. God can make you good; you choose whether you're going to be faithful or not.

"Well done, good and faithful servants"—here's what's been ringing in my mind here for three or four days. We have pastors reading this and I'm hearing back from a lot of you and am sensing that a lot of our pastors are having a discouraging time. I just want to tell you something—*stay faithful with what you have!* Well done, good and faithful servant! I have an idea that older people are reading this and your days of being productive are in the past. I want you to read this now—good and faithful, *stay faithful even in your latter years.* You can still pray and make a difference. You can give; it may not be as much, but it's just as important as anyone else's giving. You can still encourage one or two people a day. Stay faithful!

I imagine some young moms are reading this and you're doing the laundry, then you're doing the dishes, then you're fixing another meal, and then you're driving the kids here and there, and you wonder, *What in the world is all of this? All I do is just go, go, go.* "Well done, good and faithful servant!" God has given you that responsibility and those children—stay faithful!

My mom, Della Diehl, had a problem with depression in her adult life. She was hospitalized four different times and then was finally set free from that terrible disease. In one of her times of discouragement I drove to Des Moines to visit with Mom and she said to me, "Jim, it doesn't make much difference what I do or don't do. I don't have any influence. I'm not important like your dad."

I said, "Wait a minute, Mom. Wait a minute—God has given you five children. There's Donna in Chicago, there's me in Oskaloosa, there's Dorothy up in Vancouver, there's Rich down in Phoenix, and there's Kathy down in Dallas. All of your children are Christians—they're raising their kids to serve the Lord. Mom, you had five kids and they're all serving Jesus because of you, your influence and Dad's. That's what God gave you to do, in addition to a whole lot of other stuff you've done, that you're discounting. Mom, you were faithful! Look at your kids; they are now influencing hundreds of people. Mom, you're going to get the same commendation when you come to the end of life as Billy Graham—'Good and faithful servant'!"

She said, "Jim, do you really believe that?"

I said, "I *know* that!"

What are you doing with what you have been given? Stay faithful; stay faithful! That's what God wants! One thing you can do is share these thoughts with others because somebody needs to hear, "Good and faithful servant"!

God makes us good—we choose to be faithful! There's a reward coming for your faithfulness. Praise God. Bless you all!

43 DON'T LIVE LIFE LOOKING BACKWARDS

Isaiah 43:16–19

As we come toward the end of the book, it's like the end of a year. As a preacher, which I am, when I come to a day like this at the end of the year, book, or whatever, do I look back at the past or do I look forward to the future?

Well, the Lord has led me to a verse that does both—looking back and looking forward. We go to Isaiah 43, which starts out by looking backwards. This is the Jewish nation (the Jewish people), and Isaiah is reminding them of their terrible past when they were in Egypt as slaves. God miraculously delivered them, as stated in verses 16: "Thus says the Lord, who makes a way in the sea and a path through the mighty waters." Isaiah is talking about the Red Sea and that entire miracle story. "Who brings forth the chariot and horse, the army and the power" (v. 17)—that is the Egyptian army coming after the Israelites to drag them back to Egypt again. "They shall lie down together, they shall not rise; They are extinguished, they are quenched like a wick" (v. 17).

As you all well know the story, God opened a way through the Red Sea and the people of God walked across on dry ground. Then when the Egyptian army came onto that "highway in the sea," God lifted His hand, the waters came back together, and the Egyptians were extinguished. They were quenched like a wick. God was reminding the Israelites of their miraculous past as well as the terrible life they had in Egypt as slaves.

These past few years have not been miracle years for many of us. They have been very, very difficult, what with COVID-19, the economy, the unrest in America, and more. Over the past few years every one of you has experienced things that have changed, and it has not changed for the better. But I want to remind you that this ministry was born in April 2020, right at the time of the COVID-19 outbreak, because the churches had been closed and I was urged by friends and family to give these "Refuels."

Here we are, and I've heard from many hundreds of you. Let me just say that we reached between 800 and 1,200 viewers every week for fifty-nine weeks, sometimes more, and even once we had around 4,000. But the average was 800 to 1,200. That's more people than I could have spoken to if I had jumped on a plane and gone anywhere! To those of you who watched these "Refuel" times, God brought something good out of it.

I want you to read this next verse. I'm not skipping any verses now. Isaiah talked about all that I just mentioned, and he notes that God said, "Do not remember the former things, nor consider the things of old" (v. 18). He just talked about the former things; he reminded them of the miracle of their ancestors. If I could translate that to today, I would simply say, *Don't live your life looking backwards.* It's all right to look back to remember and to reflect, to rejoice, and to thank God. I'm thankful we've survived the pandemic and I'm thankful for this short time when we did the "Refuels" every week. I'm thankful for a lot of things.

In the very next verse Isaiah quotes God as saying, "Behold, I will do a new thing, now it shall spring forth; shall you not know it? I will even make a road in the wilderness and rivers in the desert" (v. 19). Obviously you can't see what I have written in my own handwriting right there after those promises, but I've written the two words *for you.* "Now I will do a new thing *for you!* I will make a road in the wilderness *for you.* I will make rivers in the desert *for you!*"

I want you to take the promises of God personally and not just leave them as promises for someone else. Personally, I feel that this is the scripture the Lord has led me to for the days ahead: "I will do a new thing *for you!*" I'm going to hang on to that one! That's the promise of God that I'm taking for me! It will spring forth—you'll see it. Thank God!

Here's what I want to say before we close. How about you? Will you ask the Lord to give you a promise for the future, to give you a word from God? Here's my verse that simply strongly states, *Behold, I will do a new thing for you. Now it shall spring forth.*

What's your promise from God? Share this with some others. Get them thinking about it. Let's get into the Word of God! I'll tell you what—we don't get much good news from the government. We'd better get to the Word and find a new promise given by God There's enough in here for all of you. God has something new for you—let's find out what it is!

God bless you. Don't live in the past. Let's look to the future. God is still in control. God is still the God of the Red Sea miracle. Claim His promise for you today!

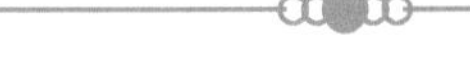

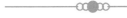

44 DELIVER ME, TEACH ME, LEAD ME, REVIVE ME

Psalm 143

Previously I have talked about healing and praying for miracles from God concerning the healing of body, mind, and soul. I'm really surprised as I reread the Psalms these days as to how many "bullet points" are put into these longer prayers that the Psalmist gives. In Psalm 143 David is pleading for God to help him because of his enemies and what they want to do to him. Right in the middle of all of that praying, we find four takeaway truths.

First, in verse 9 we read, "*Deliver me,* O Lord, from my enemies" (emphasis added). In today's culture we don't talk about people who are hard on us as our enemies. I would like to frame it like this: *Please deliver me from the people who are trying to rob my joy and my peace. They are out to steal my blessings, my peace, and my confidence.*

I had a great old friend right here in Lakewood, Colorado, who, as I noted earlier, used to say about certain people, "They know how to sandpaper you." I know the feeling. We are not praying that they will be hit by lightning or run over by a truck—"but Lord, just deliver me from them."

I have stories in which God has done it and taken care of the situation in ways that I couldn't imagine. When God does it, He does it right! That's prayer #1 from Psalm 143—*deliver me from those who are a negative, terrible influence on me.*

The next takeaway truth is in verse 10: "*Teach me* to do Your will, for You are my God" (emphasis added). That fits all of us. "*Teach me,* Lord, to know your will in my situation and the decisions that I need to make. Teach me to know, Lord, and then *do* your will!" There is no greater peace or contentment than to know that you are *in* God's will and doing His will for your life. Pray that prayer for today: "Teach me to do your will!"

The third takeaway truth is in the second part of verse 10: "*Lead me* in the land of uprightness" (emphasis added). "Lead me"—do you see it? Deliver me, teach me, *lead me.* That's a prayer we ought to be praying every day. Lead me today, Lord! Here's how I see it: when somebody leads you, he or she goes before you and you follow! You see, *you* don't lead the way and the person comes up behind you. You say, "Lord, you lead me!" That means God goes before us and then we follow! If there's something bad there, the Lord is there to take care of it. You see, God doesn't push us, He doesn't herd us like a bunch of cattle, He doesn't stampede us like a flock of sheep. He leads us! The psalmist uses that figure of speech in Psalm 23: "He leads me in the paths of righteousness" (v. 3).

Deliver me, teach me, lead me, and now for the fourth takeaway truth: "*Revive me,* O Lord, for Your name's sake!" (v. 11, emphasis added). Deliver me, teach me, lead me, and *revive me!* I like that, because we certainly need reviving! Over the last few years the COVID-19 pandemic has been hard on all of us; it's been hard on our churches. If you had revival meetings scheduled, they were probably canceled. Therefore, if we ever needed to pray that prayer, it is now: "Revive me, O Lord. Revive my soul, revive my church, revive the spirit of God in America, revive our world, O God!"

These are four takeaway truths from the middle of a pleading prayer from King David: (1) Deliver me, O Lord; (2) Teach me, O Lord; (3) Lead me, O Lord; (4) Revive me, O, Lord. I wish you would write these four truths in the back of your Bible or print them on a card and put it at the edge of the mirror you use when getting ready every morning. No matter how long you've been a Christian, you never graduate from praying those prayers. What a prayer for this day and age!

"Deliver me, teach me, lead me, revive me, O Lord." The same God who answered those prayers for King David will do the same for you! But we must pray—and obey!

45 DON'T MISS THE MOMENT

Luke 2:19–20

This chapter and the following one were done in the Christmas season and have to do with the birth of Jesus. They are placed here toward the end of the book because if you are reading one of these each week, it is now about Christmastime.

Those of you that have heard me preach from time to time may have picked up the fact that I like quotes. When I hear or read a quote that I like, I often write it in the front or back of my Bible. I've actually been known to preach a sermon or two from the back of my Bible. Here's a quote that I read last week: "You never know the value of a moment until it becomes a memory" (Dr. Seuss).

The more I think about it, the better that quote gets. I want you to read this now and I'll say it again at the very end: *Don't miss the moment!*

You talk about a moment. How about Mary and Joseph right there in Luke 2, the familiar Christmas story? The couple left Nazareth, walking, maybe with Mary riding on a donkey, all the way to Bethlehem. That's ninety miles—and Mary was ready to give birth to a baby! That's nearly an impossible journey when you're pregnant, but that's what they did, and they made it. They arrived in Bethlehem to find that the inn was full—no room. The innkeeper said, "I guess you could go in the back if you want to stay with the cattle and the donkeys." So that's what they did. They made a bed out of straw, and as you well know, the Christ child was born of Mary there in the place where the animals were supposed to be. The baby was then laid in a manger. I think we all know that a manger is where they put the hay and the other food for the animals to eat.

There the Christ child slept in a bed of straw. Out on the hillside near Bethlehem common shepherds were tending their flocks, probably bedded down because it was night. Suddenly the sky exploded in light, and an angel started speaking: "Today in the city of David a child is born." Can you imagine those shepherds? "What in the world are we seeing?" Then the sky became even brighter with a multitude of angels saying, "Glory to God in the highest and on earth peace, goodwill to men!" (Luke 2:14). The angels told them that in the city of David (Bethlehem) they would find the Christ child, the baby!

The shepherds took off, left their sheep, headed into Bethlehem, and found the inn and the stable area behind. You've got to imagine Mary and Joseph sitting quietly with their little baby in the manger when all of a sudden wide-eyed shepherds came in—and I'm sure they were all talking at once. "Man, you can't believe what we just saw! We were out there in the hills and just as we were getting ready to go to sleep, an angel started speaking and then the sky lit up and a lot of other angels appeared and started singing in the sky! We wondered what was going on!"

I think the innkeeper may have said, "Man, if these shepherds are looking for a baby, maybe I'd better see what's going on myself."

You talk about a moment—this is what is called the incarnation: God and man together in the birth of the Christ child. God had come to the world in the form of a baby born to the Virgin Mary.

This baby would live, teach, preach, heal, and set people free. Then He would die to give us a way out of our sinful lives. He paid the price on the cross of Calvary, but that's another story. All of this and more—can you just imagine?

Then the shepherds returned to the fields glorifying and praising God, for all the things that the angels had told them were true!

The Bible says that Mary kept these things and pondered them in her heart—pondered them, treasured them, soaked everything in, the whole scene that I just described. What a moment for Mary and Joseph! We're especially focused on Mary. She treasured every moment! She pondered them in her heart, and she re-lived that over and over for the rest of her life. She may have said, "I'm not missing the moment." She didn't hurry away; she didn't shove anybody out. She just soaked it in and treasured the moment.

I think of the moments in our lives, especially around Christmas. I think about the family coming back, the kids, the grandkids, and we're all gathered there in the family room on Christmas Eve with just the lights of the Christmas tree on, singing Christmas carols. In our home around the circle we would go, each person saying what God has done to help him or her in some manner that year. Then we would stand, hold hands, and pray. The tears would flow, and then we would start hugging each other, showing love to our brothers, sisters, cousins, uncles, aunts, mom, dad, grandparents—everyone. Now I see what a moment that was! Again, as Dr. Seuss said, "You never know the value of a moment until it becomes a memory."

A thought for you: the Lord turned an ordinary moment into a God moment just a few days ago for me. I was addressing Christmas cards—a lot of them—and I needed a current address. I called a friend eight or nine hundred miles away and I got the proper name and address. Then I asked, "Well, how's everything else going?" That seemed to trigger a big load she was carrying, and tears came. It was just as if this dear lady needed somebody to call and to say, "I'm going to be praying for you." According to what she said, it was just at the right moment, and I felt that little nudge to pray with her, so I just said, "Hey—let's pray before I go." On the phone that day we prayed, and there were more tears on her side and then she said these words: "God had you call me today. It was not an accident. You didn't call just for a name and address—God needed to tell me that He still cares and He's having people to step in to help me at the right moment."

Well, praise God! That was a God moment! It's not quite as dramatic as Mary and Joseph's huge moment, but it was a God moment nevertheless. I just want to say one more time: *Don't miss the moment!* Just watch, listen, and be tuned in. The Lord is going to open up something at home, on the phone, at the store, or somewhere where you need to stop and say whatever needs to be said and make the moment! To God be the glory! Merry Christmas—and *don't miss the God moment!*

46 WHOSE BIRTHDAY IS IT ANYWAY?

Matthew 1:20–23

It is Christmas week right here in Denver, Colorado, and around the world. It's one great celebration day that people celebrate worldwide. So merry Christmas to you even if you're reading this after Christmas—"Merry Christmas" is still appropriate.

I'm going all the way back to the early 1990s, which doesn't seem very far back to me, but it's actually over thirty years ago now. I was living here in Denver and saw that the Archdiocese of the Catholic Church had put up a big banner that stretched from one side of the street to the other. It was high enough that the trucks could go under it, and I want you to see this banner in your mind's eye. It said, "Whose Birthday Is It Anyway?" That made the papers, and not only did it make the papers but it also became the title of my Christmas message that year at Denver First Nazarene. My mind is now going back to that for today: *Whose birthday is it anyway?*

I want to tell you what you already know, but we need somebody to get out and say it out loud. It's not the birthday of Santa Claus, Rudolph the Red-Nose Reindeer, Frosty the Snowman, or even the little drummer boy. *It's the birthday of Jesus Christ, the Lord! It's the birthday of the Messiah, the King of kings!*

The world has tried to steal the birthday of Jesus Christ, the Messiah, with every kind of Christmas party or Christmas television special or Christmas gift-giving. I'm not saying any of that is sinful, but I *am* saying that we've become so secular that you begin thinking perhaps that Christmas is Santa Claus, Rudolph, the snowman on your lawn, the little drummer boy—but it's *Jesus!*

Let's go to the Bible, Matthew 1:20–21. Joseph and Mary had been engaged, and now they took the trip all the way to Bethlehem to register and pay taxes. An angel had spoken to Joseph to take Mary as his wife, not just to be engaged: "*Joseph, son of David, do not be afraid to take to you Mary your wife, for that which is conceived in her is of the Holy Spirit. And she will bring forth a Son, and you shall call His name Jesus, for He will save His people from their sins.»*

Here is a parenthesis: not *in* their sins but *from* their sins. Jesus came to lift us *out of* the sinful life, to live the righteous, Christlike holy life.

Then the angel quoted scripture from the Old Testament prophet Isaiah: "'Behold, the virgin shall be with child, and bear a Son, and they shall call His name Immanuel,' which is translated, 'God with us'" (Matthew 1:23). You see, the smartness, the wisdom, the ingenuity of mankind did not come together as when mankind said, "We're going to the moon. We're actually going to walk on the moon." Mankind developed a way to get to the moon, but this is not a story of mankind saying, "We need to find God, almighty God." No, this is the opposite of that. This is the holy God saying, "I'm going to build a bridge to sinful, fallen humanity. I want to walk and talk with my creation again as I originally planned it. The plan was working, but sin came and tore it all up." God built the bridge, and that bridge between a holy God and sinful man was the Son of God, Jesus Christ!

They shall call His name Immanuel . . . God with us. It is not man trying to find God. Rather, it is God coming and saying, "I have now sent Jesus. He is born as a baby. He will grow just like all the rest of you. He will learn. However, He has come to preach, to teach, to heal, to cast out demons, and He has come to die, to shed His holy blood that sins may be forgiven and that people can be united with me again in a heartfelt spiritual relationship."

Praise the Lord! Now I want to go back to Christmas. As I said, it's not Rudolph and all the rest that you see. The name even gives it away: *Christmas.* "Christ-mass!" That is what Christmas is; it was the "Christ-mass"! Have you ever heard of a birthday party in which all the guests came and brought gifts for everyone *except* the birthday boy or birthday girl? Everyone else got a gift—except the one who had the birthday! Sometimes that's the way we treat Jesus; friends, His birthday is Christ-mass!

Therefore, I want to say to you before we must come in for a landing here—Have you given Jesus something special as a gift at Christmastime? You give, everybody else gives, you may send cards, you take gifts, and you receive gifts. I just want to encourage you today to send your church a Christmas check because they proclaim Jesus Christ the Lord! Or you could send it to a Christian missionary, a Christ-preaching evangelist, or send it to a Christian mission. Since I'm in Denver I will send a check to the Denver Rescue Mission, which is a wonderful ministry group. I'll also send a check to the Salvation Army. I love them and they do great work. I just say, take care of your church first; then take care of the compassionate ministries such as the mission that is near where you live.

Whose birthday is it anyway? Jesus's! Let's honor Jesus Christ, our Lord—the bridge that came from a holy God to sinful man to bring us together again! Share this thought with others. That's a Christmas gift you could give and let them read this message one more time! It's not whether it snows on Christmas—it's that Jesus the Messiah has been born! Praise God! Merry Christmas to you all!

47 WHAT REALLY MATTERS

Philippians 1:9–10

The other day I was reading from the Holman Christian Study Bible, Philippians 1:9–10. Paul was writing to these wonderful Christians in Philippi: "I pray this: that your love will keep on growing and knowledge and every kind of discernment so that you can determine what really matters." That phrase jumped out at me, and I circled the words "so that you can determine what really matters."

There are a whole lot of things that we get all stirred up about, get stressed over, or have a meltdown over that really don't matter. Does it really matter who won the World Series last fall? (Right now I can't even remember who was in the series.) It doesn't really matter who the "final four" were last year. In the light of eternal matters, does it really matter how much Bill Gates is worth? Does it really matter who won the Super Bowl last year? In the long view of life, it doesn't really matter much who won or lost. Remember the big deal about wearing masks during the pandemic? Now, does it really matter how many months we had to do that?

I want to tell you about four things that *really* matter. Number one—your relationship with God! That affects your forever! It ultimately means heaven or hell! The Bible clearly teaches both, and in

Colossians 1:27 are some wonderful words that I want you to read: "Christ in you, the hope of glory." One's relationship with God—it is not a ritual! I'm talking about a relationship—Christ in you! Christ in me! The hope of glory!

This Christian life is not a one-and-done deal—it's a journey. It's not just "one time, make a decision, sign a card, and get on with life." No, no—it's a *journey!* It's a walk with Christ in you as you journey together. It's a lifestyle, not just a membership somewhere. I'm asking you today—do you have a personal relationship with Jesus Christ the Lord? "Christ in you"—that comes after we have repented, asked forgiveness, believed on the Lord Jesus Christ, and have been saved! Now *that* matters! That matters even if we use different words or terms about the experience. Christ in you—that matters!

The second thing that matters is your attitude toward others—toward your spouse, your family, your neighbors, your coworkers, people in general. Do you love people or do you just endure them—or even resent them? Do you respect people, or do you disrespect them? Do you live a me-first attitude? "I'll take care of me and the rest of you can do what you want." Or do you actually have true compassion and care for people? How do you treat them? If you are a Christian with Christ living in you, He says a whole lot about how we are to treat, to love, respect, and help our neighbors and friends. Are you a Good Samaritan to the person by the side of the road, a person who stops, helps, gets the person into a healing place, and prays for him or her? Now *that* really matters!

The third thing that matters is your attitude toward your responsibilities, your job, your school, your spouse, your family, your debts, your church, and the promises you make. Your attitude toward your responsibilities makes all the difference in the world! If you really have Christ in your heart, you are a promise-keeper! You give it your best on the job, at the school, and you pay your debts. There's room for a lot of preaching here, but you get the point.

What really matters when you get to the bottom line? The fourth thing that matters is your integrity, your honesty, your trustworthiness, and that can be put into one word—your *character!* Yes, that matters! In the book of Acts Luke was writing about one of those early Christians by the name of Barnabas. Read carefully this one line: "He [Barnabas] was a good man, full of the Holy Spirit and of faith" (Acts 11:24). What was Luke saying here? I checked to see what the scholars said, and they said that the Greek word for *good* could be translated "true," "pure," "stable," "reliable," "with integrity." That was Barnabas! He was a good man, an honest man, a man of integrity! That's called your *character!* That's your reputation! People have a way of trying to see if you are real or fake. I don't want to die and then people start digging around and finding all kinds of dirt about me. I want to live a genuine Christian life so there are no regrets, even after I'm gone.

I imagine if I had a thirty-minute message I could come up with ten more things that matter, but these four things for this brief thought are (1) your relationship with God, (2) your attitude toward others, (3) your attitude toward your responsibilities, and (4) your character— those *really* matter!

Let me quote the verses from the Holman Christian Study Bible one last time: "that your love will keep on growing and knowledge and every kind of discernment so that you can determine what really matters" (Philippians 1:9–10).

You *can* determine what really matters. What a powerful truth!

48 THE FOUR-LEGGED STOOL

Isaiah 7:14; Luke 1:26–27, 30–31, 35; John 1:29; Hebrews 9:14; Matthew 28:1–2, 5–7; Luke 24:31; Acts 1:4–5; 2:2–4

I've been thinking lately. . . . I've been thinking a lot lately. Possibly it's because I'm older than I used to be—but I'm thinking about things that didn't cross my mind when I was younger, reflecting on our Christian faith. What is really bedrock absolute truth that all Christians should agree on?

It's true that there are many areas where genuine Christians disagree. One is Communion, or the Lord's Supper. Should we take Communion weekly, monthly, quarterly, or just occasionally? Baptism is another. Should I be sprinkled, should the baptismal water be poured, or should I be immersed? Is it still as important as it was back in Bible days? Then there is the Sabbath day. Should we honor it on Saturday or Sunday? Women pastors are another point of disagreement. Why do some Christian denominations forbid women pastors but others openly feature women pastors and evangelists? Interesting questions! On these questions and many others not all Christians will ever agree.

Therefore, what really are the pillars of the faith? The solid-rock foundation stones that are non-negotiable? I have come up with four—therefore the title of this sermonette, "The Four-Legged Stool."

First, the incarnation, the virgin birth of Jesus Christ. The prophet Isaiah wrote some 700 years before the birth of Christ, "Therefore the Lord Himself will give you a sign: Behold, the virgin shall conceive and bear a Son, and shall call His name Immanuel" (Isaiah 7:14). Luke tells us clearly in his gospel, "Now in the sixth month the angel Gabriel was sent by God to a city of Galilee named Nazareth, to a virgin betrothed to a man whose name was Joseph. . . . The virgin's name was Mary. . . . The angel said to her, 'Do not be afraid, Mary, for you have found favor with God. And behold, you will conceive in your womb and bring forth a Son and shall call His name Jesus'" (Luke 1:26–27; 30–31).

Jesus had a human mother—her name was Mary. He did not have a human father. The Scriptures tell us, "The angel answered and said to her, 'The Holy Spirit will come upon you and the power of the Highest will overshadow you; therefore, also, that Holy One who is to be born will be called the Son of God'" (Luke 1:35). The Holy Spirit of God was the Father of Jesus. Therefore, Jesus was God-Man. Otherwise, if that is not true, Jesus was just another prophet and not the Savior. But the miracle happened, Mary became pregnant with a child, and that child was Jesus, the Savior of the world! There is no true Christianity if you take out the truth of the virgin birth! That's the first leg of this "Christian stool."

Second, the crucifixion. Throughout the Old Testament God was teaching us that there must be a blood sacrifice for sin. That's why the priests would take a spotless lamb, sprinkle its blood on the altar, and make a blood sacrifice for the sins of the people. It's not a coincidence that when John the Baptist saw Jesus, he cried out, "Behold! The Lamb of God who takes away the sin of the world!" (John 1:29). Yes, Jesus came to teach and preach about the kingdom of God and to heal all manner of diseases—but His ultimate purpose was to give a blood sacrifice for the sins of the people. That's what happened on the cross that Friday! The spotless Lamb of God was shedding His blood so that you and I could be washed clean from our sins and guilt.

Christianity is not a religion of man trying to find God. It is the story of the holy, almighty God finding a way to build a bridge of salvation to a sinful creation. That bridge was built in the form of a cross! I love Hebrews 9:14, which declares, "How much more shall the blood of Christ, who through the eternal Spirit offered Himself without spot to God, cleanse your conscience from dead works to serve the living God?" The sinless Son of God, Jesus, shed His blood on the cross to atone for the sins of everyone in Adam's race. That includes me! That includes you! Have you invited that Jesus into your heart as your Lord and Savior? The bridge has been built—but we must respond with repentance and obedience to this matchless Son of God, Jesus Christ. There is no Christianity if you take out the truth of the atonement provided at the crucifixion. That's the second leg of this "Christian stool."

Third, the resurrection. On the first day of the week Jesus Christ came out of that tomb with a resurrected body! Let's read it from the gospel of Matthew: «Now after the Sabbath, as the first day of the week began to dawn, Mary Magdalene and the other Mary came to see the tomb. And behold, there was a great earthquake; for an angel of the Lord descended from heaven, and came and rolled back the stone from the door, and sat on it. . . . But the angel answered and said to the women, 'Do not be afraid, for I know that you seek Jesus who was crucified. He is not here; for He is risen, as He said. Come, see the place where the Lord lay. And go quickly and tell His disciples that He is risen from the dead'" (Matthew 28:1–2, 5–7). The miracle of the resurrection of Jesus Christ! We now call it Easter, and Christians around the world celebrate this miracle of new life!

After the resurrection Jesus could be seen. He was recognized. He could speak. He could eat. He could walk through locked doors and appear before His disciples. He could walk along with two of His followers on the Emmaus Road, but they didn't recognize Him until "their eyes were opened and they knew Him; and He vanished from their sight" (Luke 24:31). This Jesus, who had been crucified, dead, and buried, was now very much alive! He had defeated death, hell, and the grave. Of course, it's a miracle—Jesus was the Son of God! God, not Satan, has all power! God, not Satan, will have the last word!

This resurrected Jesus wants to live in your soul and truly bring new life to you! That›s the miracle of salvation. There is no Christianity if you take out the truth of the resurrection. Jesus didn›t die as a martyr and that was the end of it. No, He was the Messiah and through the power of God He was resurrected and lives today, and He wants to live in your heart and mine. That's the third leg of this "Christian stool."

Fourth, the Holy Spirit's baptism. Before Jesus left this world and ascended into heaven, He commanded His disciples to "wait for the Promise of the Father, 'which,' He said, 'you have heard from Me; for John truly baptized with water, but you shall be baptized with the Holy Spirit not many days from now'" (Acts 1:4–5). The disciples (and many others) obeyed and waited in an upper room for some ten days. Then it happened! «And suddenly there came a sound from heaven, as of a rushing mighty wind, and it filled the whole house where they were sitting. Then there appeared to them divided tongues, as of fire, and one sat upon each of them. And they were all filled with the Holy Spirit" (Acts 2:2–4). It was traumatic! It was life changing! Fear and denial turned into power and boldness. One hundred twenty believers were all filled with the Holy Spirit and the church of Jesus Christ was born!

My friends, that was Pentecost! The disciples were Spirit baptized, Spirit filled. Everyone from Peter to the last one was changed, purified, and empowered. They started going everywhere preaching and teaching about this Jesus, who could change lives, set people free from sin, and live Christlike lives here and now.

The promise from Jesus to fill His followers with the Holy Spirit is still true today. He wants our selfish spirits to die and for us to be filled, led, and guided by His Holy Spirit. I rejoice today in the truth that we can experience the same victories that the disciples and thousands of others experienced in the early days of Christianity. There is no Christianity if you take out the power and infilling of the Holy Spirit in the hearts of His followers. That's the fourth leg of this "Christian stool."

Of course, there are many other components of what we Christians believe (from the doctrines of heaven and hell to the second coming of Christ), but these four pillars are bedrock foundational. I trust you have read my heart here today. These are not just Nazarene doctrines—these are solid-rock Christian doctrines. Let's choose to focus on what unites us Christians, not what divides us. Let's start with "the four-legged stool"—the incarnation, the crucifixion, the resurrection, and the Holy Spirit's baptism. *Jesus is Lord!*

49 SEVEN WORDS OF WISDOM, PART 1

1 Thessalonians 5:16–22

Today I want to direct you to the last part of the letter Paul wrote to the church in Thessalonica. In Chapter 5 he goes through various exhortations and theological truths. Then before he says goodbye it's as if he thought, "Wait a minute. Let me give you seven words of wisdom." I want to give you the first three today and we'll go to the other four next time.

First, *rejoice always* (v. 16). I want you to take note—he did not say, "Always be happy." I'm telling you, even when we're Christians, walking with Jesus and enjoying the blessed Holy Spirit in our hearts and lives, not all of life is just "happy, happy, happy." Bad things happen to God's good people! Christians get cancer! Christians have heart attacks. Christians have car wrecks. That doesn't make us happy, of course, but the Bible says to rejoice always!

When the hard times come, the accident happens, or the bad word from the doctor comes, we can rejoice, first, in that we don't have to go through it by ourselves. Jesus is in us and with us. Thank you, Lord—thank you that you've never failed us before, and you're not going to fail us now! Rejoice in that! Rejoice in the fact that your name is written in the Lamb's Book of Life, and if healing doesn't come, well, thank God—it is heaven forever! So I rejoice. *Rejoice always!* Again, God's Word doesn't say, "Happy, happy, happy"—but rejoice always!

Second, *pray without ceasing* (v. 17). Now how in the world can we live busy, busy lives and pray without ceasing? Here is how it has come to me as I thought about this admonition. First, it doesn't mean that we're supposed to go out and join some subgroup or a monastery or convent, walk around the park, tend to the flowers, and be in a non-stop prayer mood all day. Folks, we all live busy lives, so that's not reality—but the Word *still* says to pray without ceasing!

Here's how the Lord pictured it in my mind. You and I are taking a trip. We're in Denver, we're going to Chicago, and we're traveling in my car. We start talking to each other as we head out I-70 going east, and after a little while I say, "You know, we need to stop and get a cup of coffee. Here's a convenience station coming up—let's get off the interstate and I'll run in and get a couple of coffees and come back and give you yours and take mine." We do that, and then away we go, continuing the trip, the conversation resumes, focusing on what we were talking about before, just going on with our conversation where we left off.

Then in an hour or so I say to you, "You know, I think I really do need to take a bathroom break, so let's pull off the interstate here and let's go in here to that big truck stop coming up." We do that, we go to the restroom, you grab a candy bar, we come back to the car, and we start traveling east again. The conversation resumes: "Now you know, that's kind of a complicated thing we're talking about, but you know, I really think. . . . What do you think about that?" Then in another hour, "Hey—let's stop and get a sandwich." We do that, get back in the car, and start right back in on the conversation again.

We can live in communication with the Lord! You can start talking to the Lord when you first wake up in the morning. "I thank you, Lord, for so much. I've got this on me today and I need your help, Lord." You can pray like that while you're getting ready. You get busy and then you get to your work, or you're working at the house or you're with the kids. You have to be focused on that, but then you get a break and you say, "O Lord, thank you. We got through that one, didn't we? " You can actually pray without ceasing as a lifestyle by practicing the presence of God. You can talk to God just as you talk to your friend all the way to Chicago.

Third, *in everything give thanks* (v. 18). As Paul says, it is God's will for you in Christ Jesus. This is a big one! *In everything give thanks!* The Word does not say to give thanks *for* everything—but *in* everything. I'm not thankful for every bad thing that happens; neither is God thankful for all the sin, wickedness, and evil that's going on in our world! But *in* everything give thanks! Thank God—just as I was talking about the rejoicing, "Thank God—you're with me, Lord! I don't know how we're going to get through this, but I'm hanging on to you and you're holding on to me." *In everything give thanks.*

Rejoice, pray, and in everything give thanks! I need to tell you that something has happened to me for which I'm not thankful. You might remember that two or three years ago I had a tumor in my bladder that was cancerous and had to be surgically removed.

Another one has come back, and I've now been diagnosed with another cancerous tumor in my bladder. My good urologist said that we have to go right back to Lutheran Hospital and have surgery again. It has been scheduled for early August.

I didn't walk out of the doctor's office saying, "Well, thank you, Jesus! I've got a cancer problem again." No, no! I'm not happy about it, but *in everything give thanks.* "Lord, you walked with me through it before; you're going to walk with me through it again this time. Lord, I don't know all that's going to happen, but it's in your hands and I thank you for it."

I just want you to know that we're going to make it and we can rejoice always. Thank God that we don't have to go through dark times by ourselves. We're going to pray without ceasing and *in* everything—not *for* everything but *in* everything—we're going to give thanks.

Concerning the seven words of wisdom, three are done, with four to go. I'll see you next time as we dig further into Paul's seven words of wisdom.

50 SEVEN WORDS OF WISDOM, PART 2

1 Thessalonians 5:16–22

I started last time on the seven words of wisdom from 1 Thessalonians 5 and got through the first three: *rejoice always, pray without ceasing,* and *in everything give thanks* (not *for* everything but *in* everything.). I want to finish with the four remaining words of wisdom today. When these seven are together, they're tremendous guidance for anyone who's wanting to walk with the Lord and live the Christian life

The fourth one is *do not quench the Spirit* (v. 19). The Holy Spirit has been characterized by fire, wind, and a dove. Many churches have logos with a flame and a cross. Of course, the cross is the symbol of Jesus Christ and the flame is a symbol of the Holy Spirit. Do not quench the Spirit! If the Spirit within us is a fire, remember that water quenches fire. You pour water on fire to put the fire out. Don't put water on the workings of the Holy Spirit in your life!

Of course, disobedience to God is the fastest way to quench the spirit. Don't neglect reading the Word of God, praying, attending worship services, and fellowshipping with your fellow Christians. If we neglect these important practices, the Spirit is quenched little by little. Here the Scripture says, "Do not quench the Spirit" (v. 19). Don't put water on the fire. Don't neglect the things of God!

Fifth, *do not despise prophecies* (v. 20). In the Bible days, of course, people didn't have the whole Bible. They had the Old Testament scriptures, but they obviously did not have the New Testament as it was being written as they lived. The preachers (prophets) would prophesy (that's not only talking about what's ahead—it's "forth telling" as well as foretelling). They were giving the truths of the Word of God and as the Holy Spirit inspired them, such as in this very letter we're reading from Paul right now to the church in Thessalonica. He wrote, "Do not despise prophecies" (v. 20). I don't think you despise preaching or spiritual teaching today, but I'm going back to the word I used previously—don't *neglect.* Don't neglect Bible preaching and Bible teaching. Bible preaching feeds your soul and illuminates so you see things more clearly. Bible preaching also helps to bring conviction about things that we need to avoid. Don't quench the spirit; don't *neglect* Bible preaching.

Sixth, *test all things; hold fast what is good* (v. 21). Friends, if they needed to test things in that day, God knows we need to test things today! There's every kind of strange doctrine floating around that you can think of and we need to test them. Don't be gullible; don't believe everything you hear; don't believe everything you read. Many teachings are given for truth but are absolutely not square with the Word of God! The Word is our compass, our guide to what is truth! The Word of God has lived through centuries and will stand long after we're gone. So test against the Word of God what you hear and what you see. If it doesn't square with the Word—let it go!

Seventh, *abstain from every form of evil* (v. 22). Abstain—that means to stay away from, reject, avoid evil of every kind! You will notice that Paul here in the Scriptures did not then put out a long list of things that were evil. Times have changed; we're in a different culture and there are many different cultures around the world. Let me just say—if it's evil, if it pulls you away from God, if it hurts other people, abstain, avoid, push it away! Don't live as close to sin and evil as you can—*get as far away as you can!*

Those are the apostle Paul's seven words of wisdom. The more I have thought, studied, and prayed about the seven truths, the more I see that these seven words of wisdom will guide us straight to heaven! Rejoice, pray, be a thankful person, don't quench the Spirit (don't put water on the fire of the Holy Spirit), don't neglect Bible preaching and teaching, test everything, and run away from that which is evil! You can't beat that, can you? I wish you would do this: write in the margin of your Bible at 1 Thessalonians 5:16–22: "seven words of wisdom."

Now let's read the next two verses: "Now may the God of peace Himself sanctify you completely; and may your whole spirit, soul, and body be preserved blameless at the coming of our Lord Jesus Christ. He who calls you is faithful, who also will do it" (vv. 23–24).

This is the last Refuel chapter, and what a blessing it has been to share with you these past fifty weeks or so! I've heard from various parts of the world as well as across North America, and you have touched my heart. Thank you for being part of "my congregation," whether by video in the long months of the COVID-19 pandemic or by reading this book with these thoughts in it. If I never get to see you here on earth, I'll see you in heaven, "just inside the Eastern Gate"!

As Paul closed his letter to the Thessalonians (v. 28), I will close my visit with you: "The grace of our Lord Jesus Christ be with you. Amen."

ABOUT THE AUTHOR

JIM DIEHL could be called "Dr. Diehl" or "Rev. Diehl," but he prefers being called "*Pastor* Diehl." He has been senior pastor of five churches of the Nazarene across the years in Iowa, Georgia, and Colorado. He has also served ten years as district superintendent of two districts (Nebraska and Colorado) and as vice-president of MidAmerica Nazarene University.

In 1993 the General Assembly of the Church of the Nazarene elected him to serve as general superintendent, a position he filled for sixteen years. When he retired from that position in 2009, he had ordained just over 1,600 new ministers worldwide.

He is a graduate of Olivet Nazarene University and in 1990 Northwest Nazarene University conferred on him the doctor of divinity degree in recognition of his leadership and ministry accomplishments.

Diehl married his high school sweetheart, Dorothy, while a student at Olivet Nazarene University. Jim and Dorothy were the parents of four children: Jodi, Jim Jr., Don, and David. They were married for sixty-five years and truly were a "team in ministry." David went to heaven in 2008 because of melanoma cancer, and Dorothy moved to her heavenly home in 2021. Jim and Dorothy were also proud grandparents of seven grandchildren and ten great-grandchildren.

Pastor Diehl has laid down his administrative duties, but his passion continues with an ongoing preaching ministry from a pastor's heart. He frequently speaks at camp meetings, college revivals, ministerial and/or lay retreats, zone crusades, and international events. He continues making his home in Lakewood, Colorado.

Made in United States
Troutdale, OR
08/02/2024

A compilation of 50 readings from the heart of Pastor Jim Diehl. Through personal stories and biblical teaching, his desire is that you will find encouragement and hope for your walk with Christ.

PASTOR JIM DIEHL could be called "Dr. Diehl" or "Rev. Diehl," but he prefers being called "Pastor Diehl." He has been senior pastor of five churches of the Nazarene across the years in Iowa, Georgia, and Colorado. He has also served for ten years as district superintendent of two Nazarene districts (Nebraska and Colorado) and as vice president of MidAmerica Nazarene University.

In 1993 the General Assembly of the Church of the Nazarene elected him to serve as general superintendent, a position he filled for sixteen years. When he retired from that position in 2009, he had ordained just over 1,600 new ministers worldwide.

He is a graduate of Olivet Nazarene University, and in 1990 Northwest Nazarene University conferred on him the Doctor of Divinity degree in recognition of his leadership and ministry accomplishments.

Diehl married his high school sweetheart, Dorothy, while a student at Olivet Nazarene College (now University). Jim and Dorothy were parents of four children, Jodi Jim Jr., Don, and David. They were married for 65 years and truly were a "team in ministry." Dave went to heaven in 2008 because of melanoma cancer and Dorothy movec to her heavenly home in 2021. Jim and Dorothy were also proud grandparents of sever grandchildren and ten great-grandchildren.

Jim has laid down his administrative duties, but his passion continues with ar ongoing preaching ministry from a pastor's heart. He frequently speaks at camp meetings, college revivals, ministerial and lay retreats, zone crusades, and internationa events. He continues making his home in Lakewood, Colorado.

www.PastorJimDiehl.